# THE WRITER'S GPS

# THE WRITER'S GPS

*A Guide to Writing & Selling Your Book*

DEANNA R. ADAMS

Note to Reader: This book is designed to provide information on the craft and business of writing a book. This reference should serve as a general guide and not as the ultimate source on this vast and changing subject. This book does not cover children's writing because the author has not written or published in that category and so, does not feel qualified to cover that topic. However, much of the content here applies to these writers as well.

ISBN 13: 9781517682279
ISBN: 1517682274

**ADVANCED PRAISE FOR *THE WRITER'S GPS*:**

"Whether you're new at this game or a seasoned writer, Deanna Adams has put together a guidebook that will never gather dust on your shelf. Highly useable, useful, and full of examples, you'll reference it repeatedly. I recommend *The Writer's GPS* to every writer I coach."
Steve FitzGerald, writing coach and award-winning ghost writer

"Like a writing teacher at your shoulder, Deanna Adams helps you navigate your way through any writing project, fiction or nonfiction, with humor and common sense. Her advice on writing the perfect nonfiction proposal is clear and concise, and her ideas on creating fictional characters and dialogue that pops is spot-on. The writing exercises will help take your writing to the next level."
Casey Daniels, author of more than 50 books, including the Pepper Martin mystery series

"Like most successful writers, Deanna Adams learned her craft by steeping herself in the lessons of our finest and most inspiring writers. In *The Writer's GPS*, she passes on much of what she's learned. Best of all, she does so in the warm, encouraging, affirming voice I've come to know and love over a 20-year-plus friendship. She's the real deal."
– John Ettorre, writing and editing consultant

# ACKNOWLEDGEMENTS

No writer does it alone.

And so, I am eternally grateful to those I could not have done without during the writing of *any* of my books. They remain my faithful tribe. Thank you to my longtime Western Reserve Writers Group: Diane Taylor, Aileen Gilmour, Nancy Piazza, Karen Fergus, Karen Peterson, Cheryl Laufer. And my Ah-Roma Writers' Group: Carole Calladine, Barbara McDowell, Anne McFarland and Anne Bruner. You ladies are my rock. And my best friends.

I wish to thank those who took the time to read this book and write such nice endorsements: Casey Daniels, John Ettorre, and Steve FitzGerald—you are my literary heroes. Thanks to Karen Duvall of Duvall Design for the awesome cover. And thank you, Chad Ely of Ely Multimedia Group, for getting me through a computer hack just before printing time—you saved the day, or rather, this book!

I am also grateful to my family and friends, and those I've had the pleasure to become friends with through social media. I love your positive energy, great comments, and "Likes." You are all responsible for my bad habit of being on Facebook too much—and yet you so often make my day!

As always, to my family—my awesome daughters, Danielle and Tiffany, my even more awesome granddaughter, Zoey, and my husband, Jeff, who's been there all along this crazy ride. Thank you all for your love and support.

Finally, to all the struggling writers out there, I hope this book gives you the information, inspiration and incentive to accomplish what you need to write that dynamite book of your dreams!

# TABLE OF CONTENTS

# INTRODUCTION

*"The writer is an explorer. Every step is an advance into a new land."*
*- Ralph Waldo Emerson*

One day in 1999, after completing my first book, I was talking with an acquaintance (let's call her Mary) about my experience and how excited I was to be at the end of the four-year project. The conversation went something like this:

"You know, I always wanted to write a book," Mary said, a touch of envy in her voice. "In fact, I have a great idea for one. I want to write about being a soccer mom. People don't realize how much it involves! The time, the money, the anxiety of wins and losses."

"Sounds good," I said. (This was before the term "soccer moms" became a cliché.) "Books on parenting and sports are always popular, and the combined angle should be of interest to parents who are experiencing, or about to experience, the same thing."

"Yeah, I tell you, it's exhausting," Mary added. "I feel like it's taken over my life."

"That's why it's a good idea!" I said, anxious to encourage her. "You can address how an overwhelmed parent can manage the demands and survive a child's love of a sport."

I was off and running. "First, you need to do some research. Find articles that have been written on the topic, then check what other books are out there, so you know your competition. That'll give you some idea on how you want to approach it.

"Once you've done that," I continued, "draft an outline, a proposed table of contents, and have a snappy working title. You might want to start off with your personal story. How you became a soccer mom, and how it's consuming your life. Include stories of other moms, too, and how the commitment can affect the whole family . . ."

I was on a roll.

"Then start interviewing those moms and, of course, the coaches. You'll also want to talk to the kids. Get their opinions about what it's like from their point of view. And even though it's about moms, include the dad's take on it as well. After all, it's a family situation and they need to be supportive, too. And *make sure* you tape every interview!

"After that, you can begin the actual writing," I said, a little breathlessly. "Give yourself a targeted word count each day. Start with maybe 500 words, then increase it as you go. You'll find . . ."

That's when I noticed my friend's glazed eyes, like a store mannequin's empty stare. I thought I might be going too fast (and she wasn't taking notes, which I was about to suggest), so I paused. "Oh, sorry, did you have a question?"

Her eyes widened.

She rose her hand like a traffic cop. "Whoa, hold on," she said, shaking her head. "I didn't want to go through all that work! I just wanted to write a book!"

And there it was. The cold, hard truth. The difference between those who do and those who don't. I realized then that some people—dare I say, many—think this writing-a-book thing is as easy as making toast. I'm reminded of this story every time I teach my class, "What It Takes to Write a Book." It's a three-week course that ends up being only one week for those like Mary.

Many people, and maybe you, too, believe that all a writer has to do is sit at the keyboard, pound out words, then watch the royalties roll in. Nearly every aspiring writer with a "good idea" dreams of being the next Stephen King, James Patterson, or Nora Roberts. But even *they* had to work hard for their success. Remember, to become an author, you must first become a writer. Like any other field of study, you must learn the craft, know the business, live the life. Fortunately, that is possible. No matter what your age, background, or life experience, you *can* learn to become a good writer.

That's the good news.

Here's the bad: Writing, and completing, a book is a lot like boot camp. If you're not disciplined and determined, you won't make it past the first few months. It has to start, and end, with you. In order to accomplish this goal, you must be committed to see your work through, to work hard at your craft, invest your time.

That said, if you love the art of writing, it shouldn't be too hard. You should enjoy the process, along with the challenges you'll meet toward your ultimate goal. If you have a passion for your subject, you'll get great satisfaction watching your creative idea turn into something concrete.

Writing a book is a lot like a marriage. There's the Honeymoon phase, when we bask in the newness and excitement of it all, wearing rose-colored glasses, and thinking that everything will be fun and wonderful. Then comes the Trenches phase, when reality sets in, and we start to wonder if we've made the right decision, doing the right thing. That's when the real work begins. We must adjust to unexpected situations, find out how we can make improvements. If we are lucky, we make it to the Milestone phase. The work is done, and we get to have a party. For writers, instead of an anniversary party, we get to host a book launching party. We can bask in the joy of accomplishment and celebrate with family and friends!

*The Writer's GPS: A Guide to Writing & Selling Your Book* is your navigation for success. In this book, you'll find the guidance, information, inspiration, publishing and marketing tips that will turn your dream into reality. It is your personal vehicle that will get you from point A to point Z, steering you to your destination as a published author.

Welcome to the first day of the rest of your writing life.

# Part One—Write It

*"Writing well means believing in your writing and believing in yourself, taking risks, daring to be different, pushing yourself to excel. You will only write as well as you make yourself write."*

\- William Zinsser, author of On Writing Well

*Chapter 1*

# RULES OF THE ROAD: WHAT WRITERS NEED TO KNOW

*"Get it down. Take chances. It may be bad, but it's the only way you can do anything really good."*
*– William Faulkner*

Most writers don't wake up one morning and suddenly think, "I'm going to write a book." The decision to write a book often originates from a vague idea, which then stays stored in the brain for some time. It often remains just a dream until something sparks the process, like a New Year's Eve resolution, milestone birthday, or flat-out determination.

Before you begin this journey, or shall I say adventure, there are a few things to consider. First, know that writing a book is an investment. A commitment that will take time and thought and hard work. Will it be worth it? That depends if, in fact, it is a good book idea—and that you can write it. Here's how to know.

## Ask Yourself These Questions:

1. Are you an avid reader? Do you want to write books similar to your favorites?
2. Do you have a passion for a particular topic and feel a great need to write a book about it?
3. Why is the topic, or genre, important to you?
4. Do you want to document your family stories, or tell your personal life story? Why?
5. Would the book's theme be of interest to others?
6. Do you love digging into a project? Are you good at seeing it through?
7. Do you know exactly where your book would fit into the market-place? What genre?
8. Do you have an overwhelming desire, and need, to be a published author?

These are all good reasons to write a book. And knowing *why* you want to write it is a good step toward achieving it. Also, write the kind of book you love to read. Because that's where your passion lies. You will need that passion to get through the rough patches, the stumbling blocks, the difficult passages, that are part of writing a good book.

In terms of future marketing, you need to know if your book idea/theme is something that will interest a large number of people. After all, you want people to read it, buy it. And for that reason, you'll want to make sure this book turns out to be the best it can possibly be.

Now, how do you begin?

## THE SECRET FORMULA

Okay, here it is:

There is none.

Like the perfect diet, we all wish there was a fast, easy way to accomplish our goals. But what it always comes down to is plain old hard work and discipline. Sorry to be a Debby Downer, but that's the long, hard truth of it. So if you've decided that this is your time to write that book, there are some key elements to remember.

**The Purpose of Any Book Is:**

* To Educate and Inform. Or . . .
* To Enlighten (make readers aware of something they didn't know). Or . . .
* To Entertain (and then you must!)

Keep focused on the reason you are writing this book. One question you need to ask throughout the entire process is *Who Cares?* Your readers certainly should. There must be a reason your audience will want to read—and finish—your book. They want to get hooked to the story on the first page and stay engaged—until the last word.

**Steadfast Rule:** Always keep your reader in mind as you write.

## WHAT WRITERS NEED TO KNOW – TIPS FOR SUCCESSFUL BEGINNINGS

You are sitting at the keyboard, ready to let the words flow. You're inspired by a book you've just read or a movie you can't get out of your head, and you decide this is it. It's time to get down to business. You want to write a good story, fiction or nonfiction, and have carved out the time in your busy schedule to do just that (tips in Chapter 2).

But now all your insecurities (can I really do this?), nagging questions (how long should it be? What to leave in, what to leave out?), and creative decisions (grammar issues, word choices, beginnings, middles and endings—Oh My!) have surfaced. You suddenly realize that time management is not your only hurdle. Just thinking about all that goes into the makings of a book is overwhelming. And scary.

Okay, deep breath. Try not to imagine the whole book. Take it one chapter at a time. Like any 12-step program. One day, one passage, at a time. Once you understand that, and a few other things, the process will be easier to absorb.

First step: Make a sign to hang above your computer screen, or next to your keyboard, or post somewhere on your writing desk:

**Today is the First Day of the Rest of My Writing Life.**

This will remind you to get going, that time can be easily wasted away. Below that sentence add: **Do Not Check Email, Twitter, Facebook, Pinterest, etc. During Writing Time!**

Next: On a wall in your work space, hang another sign that reads:

*"Every morning I am handed 24 golden hours. They are one of the few things in this world I get free of charge. If I had all the money in the world, I could not buy an extra hour. What will I do with this priceless gift? I must use it as it is given only once. Once I waste it, I can never get it back."* – Anonymous.

Let this be your mantra.

**Here are some fundamental rules you should know about being a writer:**

1. **Forget what you learned in high school English** (well, okay, not all of it).

Nowadays, interesting writing is less stilted, less formal. You still need to be grammatically correct, of course, but your writing should be conversational, and flow easily from one sentence, one paragraph, to the next. Yes, you *can* "end a sentence with a preposition." Or begin a sentence with a conjunction, such as "And" or "But." And by all means, feel free to use fragments! A fragment, even just one word standing alone, is a great way to emphasize a particular emotion or character's thoughts, and create tension.

There is a time and place in which to break these old, die-hard rules, but don't be sloppy. And don't overdo it. The purpose is to help the prose read more smoothly. Learn how and when to break those rules by reading other books (by good authors, of course) and see how they do it. You learn a lot by reading great works.

2. **Begin your first sentence, first paragraph, first page, with a "Hook."**

A hook is the "pow." A sentence, or sentences, that grab the reader's attention. You know how the hook works, even if you haven't heard the term. Look at the first pages of your favorite books. Notice how the author hooked you into the story. It's not always a dramatic moment, but it's always something that gets the reader interested or emotionally involved. That's the key. That's the Hook.

Here are two examples of a beginning of a story:

"Homeless people really kind of fascinate me. The other day I was in a taxicab that had stopped for a red light. It was a long red light so I looked down at my dress wondering if I had made the right decision. Was it fancy enough for this occasion? Maybe I should have gone with the blue one that I'd first chosen. I shrugged, *well, too late now*. The light was still red so I looked out the window, and that's when I saw a messy looking woman rooting through a dumpster. I watched her as she leaned further into the can, looking for some kind of treasure. But then, a treasure to us regular people would be totally different than one this lady might view as a treasure. So I'm looking and wondering, why don't these people just get a job? Then, just as the light turned green, I noticed the woman actually looked kind of familiar and I thought . . ."

"I was sitting in a taxi, wondering if I had overdressed for the evening, when I looked out the window and saw Mom rooting through the Dumpster." - From *The Glass Castle,* Jeannette Walls.

Which story would you rather read? And why? You'll notice in the first example, it takes a long time—and a lot of unnecessary details and adverbs (really, totally, actually)—to get to the point, which is the unexpected, and striking, appearance of the author's mother. Had Walls begun her memoir like the first example, she probably would never have found a publisher for her story. *That's* how important that first page is.

The first example shown is called, "purple prose." When the description is too long, too wordy, or just plain too much, whereas a shorter version would kick start the story in a grander, more immediate fashion. Like the second example. Which is quick, concise and captivating (Hemingway was The Master at this—study his works). Most important, it creates an emotional response: the image of a grown woman seeing her elderly mother rooting through a dumpster.

Hook the reader with that first intriguing sentence, that first intriguing page. The beginning of a story should do many things: Introduce the main character (fiction or nonfiction), show conflict/story problem, create a vivid image, and set the tone for the remainder of the book (is it a suspense story? Humorous? Romantic? Poignant memoir?). From that first page, the reader should know what kind of story it is. Make the reader care what is happening, and wondering what will happen next.

3.  **Read, Read, Read.**

    In his book, *On Writing*, Stephen King says, "If you don't have the time to read, you don't have the time, or tools, to write." So true. Reading will give you the tools you need to learn what works. And I'll take that premise and add this: Read books in the genre that you want to write. Each genre has its own rules. For example, romance novels always end happily, with the man and woman coming together—at last!

Pay attention to how the story is constructed, how it draws you in from that first page and keeps your attention and interest. Notice the use of dialogue, description, scene, character development, etc. Also, study books on writing. Take time to read the books that will inspire you, educate you through their prose, and ultimately make you a better writer.

4. **Get it all down first**.

Anne Lamott calls it "shitty first drafts" for a reason. Beginnings are all about getting the words, the story, down. There will be many drafts to come. And the story *will* change as you write. *Don't worry about it.* You have to have something on the page first before you can X it out, change it up. Write and keep writing.

You can write the whole book without editing as you go, but I like to edit it chapter by chapter so I don't have so much work during the second draft. However, while that works well with nonfiction, with fiction, it might slow down the story and cause problems. Try to get the whole storyline down first. The story should always come before worrying about the editing and revision process.

When you feel a chapter is ready for another look, print it out. Then read it out loud, red pen at the ready. Cut out the fat, those "weasel" words—extra non-descriptive words you don't need—like *very* and *just* (more examples at end of chapter). Delete the boring narratives that don't advance the story. The fancy three or more syllable words when one will do. If you can't seem to "kill your darlings," put them in a separate file, if that makes you feel better. But get that "stuff" out of your prose's way.

5. **Trust the process and understand it.**

Producing a good piece of writing takes work. And time. And revisions. You learn by doing. And doing over. Don't be in a hurry to "just get it done and out there." Realize and accept that it's going to take as long as it takes. So that when it's finally done, your book will be something you can be proud of.

6. **Hang out with other writers.**

Remember what your mother used to say: "You are who you associate with." Want to be a writer, author? Spend time with them. Get into their circle. You need the camaraderie. No one understands, nor cares, about the challenges of being a writer more than those who actually do it. Writers will tell you about places to go, upcoming events, classes for writers, authors to see, books to read—and it all helps improve your craft. Learn from those who accomplish, produce. Go to author book signings, author fairs and pick their brains: Ask them what inspired their books, how they went about writing it, how they got through the hurdles, how they overcame it all. Most don't mind a bit, especially if it's a slow signing. They will welcome the conversation, and you'll welcome getting some food for thought.

7. **Invest in yourself and your craft.**

Take classes, attend workshops, conferences, and retreats. Whether you are an aspiring writer, or have written and published for years, there's always more to learn. Always need for improvement. Always someone who knows more than you. Always new ways to promote your work.

8. **You should be having fun.**

Writing a book is hard work, no doubt. But you won't get through it if you are not having fun. If you're writing a nonfiction book, you should enjoy the research, have fun discovering more about your subject. You should love interviewing the fascinating sources you'll be quoting in your book. If you're writing fiction, have fun making up a new world. Fall in love with your characters (if you don't, your readers won't either), or at least find them captivating.

Relish the pure act of writing and watching your story idea grow into an actual book!

## SO ... DO YOU HAVE WHAT IT TAKES?

When I started to write my first book, *Rock 'n' Roll and the Cleveland Connection*, I didn't know if I had what it took to write a book. Not Really. Although I'd been a freelance writer for years, I wasn't sure I could write a whole book. By myself! What I did know was that I was obsessed with the topic and couldn't wait to wake up every morning and work on it. And that, my up-and-coming authors, is sometimes all it takes. Enthusiasm and passion for your book. Like falling in love, desire can be a great motivator.

### Writing Exercise:

As you begin writing your book, be careful of the "weasel" words you use. These are the adjectives, adverbs and unnecessary words that don't add anything to the prose. After writing a new chapter of your story, use the "Find" feature in your computer to see how many of these words you have used, and how many times you have used them. You might be surprised. Here are some of the most common:

**Very**
**Just**
**So**
**Really**
**Quite**
**Rather**
**Literally**
**Totally**
**Completely**
**Truly**
**Perhaps**
**Maybe**

This is a good exercise to make you more aware of how often we use these terms. It is not to say, however, that you will never see them in well written books, or that I never use them in this book, as you will see. You'll also find them in the quotes used by famous writers. The objective is to be aware of *when* and *how* you use them. If the sentence reads fine without them, delete. If the word seems necessary to emphasize your point better, go ahead. Just don't overuse. That said, you absolutely *can* use these words in dialogue if your character talks that way.

But be sparse.

**Writing Workshop:**
Try the **NaNoWriMo** approach. **Even if it's not November.**

NaNoWriMo means National Novel Writing Month and it's a great way to learn how to be disciplined and keep consistent in the act of writing. The premise is to write an entire book in the month of November, with the end goal to produce a 50,000-word novel. If you're writing nonfiction, you can still try the word count challenge. It's about the discipline of writing every day and setting goals, as discussed in Chapter 2.

For details on this writing project, see www.nanowrimo.org

*Chapter 2*

# ROAD MAPPING: SETTING & MEETING YOUR WRITING GOALS

*"The key is not to prioritize what's on your schedule,
but to schedule your priorities."*

*- Stephen Covey, author of The 7 Habits of Highly Effective People*

I have a friend who is a great storyteller. I met her when I joined my first writers' group, twenty years ago. She was working on a wonderful mystery novel that had us all hooked from the first page. Every month at our group meeting, we looked forward to reading more of the story, and ultimately find out who "done it."

We are still waiting.

No, she didn't quit the group. She just got another story idea. Then, another one. Soon, another one . . . you get the drift. My friend has probably started more than ten book-length (or would be) works-in-progress since I've known her. All good books. All incomplete.

She's not the only one, not by a long shot. The unfortunate part of being a creative type is that inspiration often gets in the way of production. We all love the romance of the early start of a book, but then it becomes real work, and well, it's all too easy to "put it aside" and start that exciting *new* book idea!

If you are guilty of this kind of stagnation, do not despair. After all, that's why you bought this book, right?

Okay, here's the thing. Sometimes it's good to put a manuscript aside in favor of one that seems to offer more promise. Maybe there is good reason it's not getting finished. Perhaps it's more of a short story than a full-length book. Maybe it just doesn't "have legs," as they say. Or maybe, *maybe*, it's not as good as you thought. I know, hard to admit. But better to realize it now than go through all that work only to discover it later, right?

Then again, the book might indeed be good, but you're getting overwhelmed with the knowledge that it needs to be better—as great as you first imagined it to be. It has become hard work. You know this because when you sit to write, you decide to first check your email, peek in on Facebook to catch up with friends, do some laundry, play with your cat, pay a bill or two . . . You find that writing this book isn't as much fun anymore.

That's your clue that it's time to amp up the story. If *you* become bored with the book, it's a guarantee your readers will feel the same way. So make something happen!

How? Try these ideas:

* Veer from the original storyline. Your initial outline or proposed chapters are how you envisioned the plot before you started, before it became *real*. Once you get deeper into the story, things happen. The structure changes, characters evolve . . . it becomes a bit different from what you originally envisioned. And that's okay. If nonfiction, try and tell the story in a different way, from a different vantage point, point of view. If fiction, maybe the characters aren't interesting enough, or there's not enough action. When your story starts swerving into a new direction, go ahead and see if that course makes for a better story. Many times it does. Go with it.

* Bring in a new character, create a new problem. Something exciting needs to happen in your story to keep the reader (and you) from getting bored or losing interest. We all want to be entertained when we read. Even if it's a learning manual.

* Don't give up just because the going gets tough. That's all part of the process and that's what separates those who do from those who don't.

Of course, sometimes the problem is not the story, but the writer. In order to write, rewrite, and *finish* your book, you need to know how to accomplish your goals. You need to organize your life, stay focused on that book, and maintain your enthusiasm!

**REMEMBER THIS QUOTE:** Norman Vincent Peale said: "The greatest power we have is the power of choice. Right now you are living your past choices. Where you are today—at this very moment—is the result of your past decisions."

Think about it. The **decisions** you make today will be your **experiences** tomorrow. If you want to be that published author signing copies of your books in front of a line of readers, first you need to know the difference between a **DREAM and a GOAL**:

**Dreams** are illusionary. **Goals** are concrete. **Dreams** are Make Believe. **Goals** are Making Plans. And we really can't have one without the other. Dreams are what first provides us the inspiration and vision for what we ultimately want. **Goals**, in turn, gives us the motivation and organization to make it happen. Once that goal is achieved, we feel a wonderful sense of satisfaction—until we move on to the next goal, which starts the chain over again, prompting more achievements!

Here are a few examples of people who worked hard at their **Goals** to become the successful writer of their **Dreams:**

**Writer Anne Lamott** was a clerk/typist who wrote every night for an hour, and though she received her share of rejections, she kept writing because she could not *not* write.

**Novelist John Grisham** began by subscribing to *Writer's Digest* magazine, then wrote chapters of his first novel while riding every morning on the subway to his job as a lawyer.

**Novelist Elizabeth Berg** was a nurse and mother of small children in 1984 when she began writing for her small town newspaper. Soon after, she submitted an essay contest to *Parents* magazine – and won $500. She started publishing regularly in national magazines, then went on to write her first of many successful novels.

**Prolific romance novelist, Nora Roberts,** was "one of the worst secretaries ever!" But she always loved stories and soon found she had a knack. A simple act of nature - a snowstorm - prompted her first book, published in 1981. Since then, she has written more than fifty novels, some under the pseudonym of **J. D. Robb** for her suspense thrillers.

**Memoirist Mary Karr** had a childhood that certainly didn't lend itself to a successful life, yet wrote her memoir (in an era when publishers said you best be a celebrity if you want to sell your memoirs) so brilliantly that her first book, *The Liars' Club*, became the bar in which creative nonfiction writers aspire to.

**J.K. Rowling's** brilliant Harry Potter series was rejected by twelve publishing houses (and you can bet they now regret that decision), but she didn't quit. Today her name is mentioned among all the other great writers of the century.

**Kathryn Stockett** wrote a book that received rejection after rejection. Her worst one was number 40, which read, "There is no market for this kind of writing." She cried, but kept sending it out because "I couldn't let go of *The Help*." Finally, after 20 more rejections, the 61st publisher accepted her book, which became an international bestseller, and made into a highly successful movie.

If you are unfamiliar with the works of these authors (and remember, these are a mere few of many successful ones), get a hold of their books—and other great works—and study them. How did the author get you involved from that first sentence on? How did he or she use dialogue, characterization, plot, and setting to keep you turning the pages?

Learn from the best.

**Here are a few good traits that I feel are necessary for any writer.**

I call them the Three P's:

* **Preparation**
* **Perseverance**
* **Professionalism**

Okay, there is a fourth: **Prayer**—As in "*Please* have the editor/agent or publisher accept my work!"

Now print out the following section and tape it on the wall in front of your computer, or somewhere at your desk. This should get you through those challenging days.

## TOP TEN TIPS FOR ACHIEVING YOUR WRITING GOALS

1. **Know the Difference between a Dream and a Goal.** A *Dream* is an undefined, often unrealistic, vision (like winning the lottery). A *Goal* is something that can be attainable—*when* you apply the necessary steps toward achieving it.

2. **Be Prepared.** Have one place in your home where you write and do nothing but write. This helps trigger the creative process. Also, try and keep the same writing schedule. Same time. Same place. Every day. You'll be amazed how easy the words will flow as a result of consistency.

3. **Manage Your Time.** Give yourself permission to write. No more excuses. Get up an hour earlier. Or stay up an hour later. Give yourself a word count goal every day. Even if it's 500 words a day (which is just two double-spaced pages). Make writing your priority. There is always room for a measly 500 words a day. Cut down on your TV watching. Television rarely enhances one's life and it will not make you a writer. Keep social media less social. It does have its place, but save it for when you need a break from writing, or when you're ready to promote your book. Even then, set a timer—get in, get out. I, myself, find Facebook interesting and fun, and it's a great way to stay connected with family and friends far away. As disciplined as I am, I'm not immune to its attraction, and have found that I can lose precious writing time as a result. (Thus the timer.) And though email is a necessity for most businesses these days, or to keep in touch with people, write your designated pages *before* you go into your Inbox in the mornings. Or, if you write at night, stay offline so you don't get distracted. Delegate the housework/yardwork. Have children at home? Give them daily/weekly, jobs that allow you more time to write. If you don't have children, hire a teen who could use extra money. Or give those tasks to your, hopefully supportive, partner in life.

4. **Learn your Craft. Take Classes. Attend Writers Conferences/ Workshops.** Invest in yourself and your career. Everyone needs that proverbial shot in the arm: the encouragement, stimulation, education, and camaraderie you can get from others who share your passion and teach you how to improve as a writer. Think you can't afford a writers' conference? Yes you can! It's easier than you think. Put away $5, $10, or more if possible, each week in an envelope marked, "To Become a Better Writer," in anticipation toward the next conference you'd love to attend. Some conferences offer Early Bird prices so take advantage of

that and register in time. It is at these conferences, or in those classes, that you'll meet other writers who will become cherished colleagues. Like any industry, it does help to know people in the business!

5. **Join a Writers' Group.** At conferences and other writer events, you are bound to meet others who belong to a writers' group. As you chat with them, find out who is involved in a critique group and ask if you can join. *Or* form your own. Gather those who live nearby, and plan to meet at a local coffee shop or restaurant once a week, or once a month. Everyone wants, and needs, helpful suggestions about their work and a group that meets regularly is a godsend to any writer. Not only will work-shopping make you a better writer, the regular meetings force you to be disciplined. After all, if you want feedback on your work, you must get some pages written before the next meeting!

6. **Network Whenever Possible.** Surround yourself with successful people. Meet them by attending their book signings or talks, and join their Facebook page (any writer worth their words has a FB page nowadays). Find opportunities to chat with them about their work. Writers love to share their stories. Learn from them. Stalk them (well, don't go to their house. Or call them at home. Be respectful of their time and privacy). Learn how they manage to accomplish what they do. Attend any classes they may be offering. Become part of that world and you'll be known as a writer, too, in no time.

7. **Have Literary Heroes.** You can glean much knowledge from reading great books. How did they hook you into the story from page one? How did they end a chapter and begin a new one that kept you reading? What is it about their stories that make you want to read everything they write? Reading those works keeps you excited about the art and teaches you how to do it, too. If you want to be like those authors, model their success. I've learned much about writing from my own literary heroes, which include (but not limited to) Mary Karr, Anne Lamott, John Jakes, Ray Bradbury, J. R. Moehringer, Elizabeth Berg, William Zinsser, David Sedaris, F. Scott Fitzgerald and Ernest Hemingway—each for different reasons. Who are yours?

8. **Understand You'll Need to Pay Your Dues.** That's how we learn and grow. There is not one successful writer out there who has not known rejection. The difference is what they did afterward—they've learned from it and DID NOT GIVE UP! If you're lucky, your rejection letter will include a personal note from an editor or agent giving a tip or two on how to improve the piece, or just some encouragement about your writing. It does happen, and can help drive you forward with fresh new incentive.

9. **Review your Goals Now and Then, and Revise if Necessary.** You may get halfway through a novel or researching a book and decide it's not working. By all means, drop it and begin something else. Extend your personal deadline if you need to. Revise your table of contents. Things change. You change . . . it's okay.

10. **Celebrate Your Achievements.** Celebrate after finishing a book chapter or get an article accepted, or, especially, when you get a YES! from an agent. Go out and buy yourself something (another book?). Go to the movies. Enjoy a good meal at your favorite restaurant. Sip a chocolate martini, or drink of your choice. The point is, writing is hard work and you deserve to treat yourself!

**Here's an added Tip: Believe in Yourself!** Remember, if you love the writing process, then you're already good at it. No one willingly does something they're bad at because there's no joy in it. You feel the joy by loving what you do—which makes you want to do it more . . . which makes you accomplish more . . . which results in . . . TA DA - Success!

*Just remember, you must practice in order to get better!

### *BUT WHAT IF . . .*

Life gets in the way?

And it certainly does, doesn't it? Writing a book often takes a back seat to employment demands, child-raising, family or other personal obligations.

You'll need to incorporate your writing schedule into your life—such as getting up early, or staying up later to write.

Of course, there are days when even that doesn't work. There are often everyday distractions that worm, or rather *plow*, their way in, and it seems like your book is always getting pushed aside to make way for unexpected situations. Don't let it. You must make your book a priority. Just like eating, sleeping, working, *breathing*.

Here's how to write, even when "life gets in the way."

* **Set Deadlines**. I learned to stay organized years before I set out to write my first book. As a journalist and freelance writer, it was my job to meet deadlines—or else I wouldn't get paid. It's all about organizing your time (Refer back to Tip #3), and rewarding yourself after each milestone, no matter how small.

* **Pay yourself after meeting each deadline**. Yes, as if you are your own employer. Pay yourself something after completing your word-count goal for the week, or finish a chapter, essay or short story. You can pay yourself in cash—to stuff in that envelope mentioned earlier, saving for a writers' event. Or it could be another kind of reward. Chocolate, wine, day at the movies, shopping spree, whatever makes you feel good.

## COPING WITH DISTRACTIONS

One sure way to avoid life's distractions is to go somewhere where the likelihood is minimal. Writing at home often presents challenges. Roommates, children, pets, spouses can all disturb your thought process. There's also the ringing of doorbells, or home phone. Sometimes the distraction may be you—you might be tempted to turn on the TV, go into Twitter, or Facebook, or procrastinate by doing house or yard chores, all to avoid the work of writing that book.

My current home distractions are a dog who barks at anything passing the house, a cat who insists on sitting directly in front of my computer monitor (and gets snarly when I try and move him), and a retired husband who is in and out of the house throughout the day. So when I need quiet to work on a troubling chapter, or focus on that all-important story climax, I head to the library. It's close to home and is the best, most tranquil place for me when desperately seeking writing shelter.

On the other hand, I have a friend who needs noise around her to write. She prefers the ambient din from inside a coffee shop or restaurant. The clatter of whirling blenders, banging of pots and plates and lively conversations are just the thing that gets her creative mind racing.

Determine what works for you and make it part of your schedule and routine. The main goal is to get those pages written.

## A FEW WORDS ON WRITER'S BLOCK

I don't believe in writer's block. Why? Because even when you're not at the keyboard, you're writing in your head, right? How many times have you woken in the night with great thoughts for your book? Or think of a perfect phrase while you're driving in your car? Or rush to get out of the shower because you've just thought up a great scene to propel your story forward?

When that happens you must make sure to get it down, because those thoughts are elusive. Trust me on that. Catch it like a fishing net and get it into the bucket before it squirms away. While I don't recommend using the phone while driving, you can pull over and jot those thoughts down with pen and paper, or record into your phone or a digital voice recorder.

This is why writer's block should never happen. Because when you do get time to write, you'll have plenty of notes from when you weren't at the keyboard to use when you are.

**Writing Workshop:**

**Document Your Goals and Continued Progress in a Goals Notebook—with a timeline.**

Manage your progress in a personal logbook. Writing out your goals helps you define them. Keeping track of your progress helps you stay motivated. Write out your daily, weekly, and monthly writing goals, plus any other notes you want to make, such as your personal rewards if you meet your goal for that week, month. Write whatever you want in this progress journal. Everything that you think is doable, and will keep you inspired. Most important, include a daily word count. How many words can you shoot for in a day? How much are you actually getting written each day? How can you squeeze in an extra half hour in order to meet that daily target? Start with modest numbers and increase as you go.

Think about this: Even if you start out writing just one page (approximately 250 words) a day for five days, that's 1, 250 a week, which adds up to

5,000 words approximately a month, which becomes 60,000 words a year. That is a complete or nearly complete book! Every day you can see your progress towards your goal and making it happen.

And here is a promise: This writing a book thing is addictive. Once you get immersed in the story, you'll be so pumped up watching it grow and build into something tangible, you'll have no trouble meeting—and surpassing—that original modest word count. You'll be hooked on your book!

That, my fine author friends, is how you get it done.

*Chapter 3*

## DRIVERS, PASSENGERS & HITCHHIKERS: CREATING CREDIBLE CHARACTERS

*"I try to create sympathy for my characters, then turn the monsters loose."*
*- Stephen King*

When it comes down to it, in most books, other than self-help and reference, it really is all about the characters, be it fiction or nonfiction. Without them, there isn't much of a story. Readers won't care what happens if the situation doesn't involve people, or aliens, or vampires, or witches . . .

*Characters.*

There are those who drive the story (protagonists), those who ride along as passengers (supporting or minor characters), and those who hitch a ride, often resulting in unexpected turns or major problems throughout the journey.

Readers want, and need, to get into the character's good, bad, and the ugly psyche in order to feel engaged in the story. They are anxious to get emotionally invested, to feel some kind of intimacy with the character, be able to relate to him or her in some way.

In memoir, this is imperative because it's not just your *life* that needs to be interesting, it's you as a person, a *character,* as well as the other characters from your life that you'll be putting on the page. Readers want to care what happened to you, and why it matters.

In fiction, readers want to believe in the characters, and imagine that they are real. They want to experience what the character is experiencing and feeling, be it love, hate, shock, pain, anger, fear, or joy.

Characters get us involved in the story. That's why it's necessary to introduce your main character, the protagonist, on the first page so we get hooked into his or her life struggles. Consider the six basic questions in journalism when introducing your protagonist: ***Who*** (name, persona), ***What*** (what does he want? Motivation), ***When*** (when is the story taking place? Era), ***Where*** (where is the story taking place? Setting), ***Why*** (why is he acting like he is? Why does he want what he wants so badly?), ***How*** (how did he get this way? How is he going to resolve the story problem, or will it get resolved for him?).

Notice the Who comes first. There's a reason for that. No matter how good the plot and storyline is, if we don't care, or aren't intrigued by the main character, we don't read much further than Chapter One. If that.

If you are writing nonfiction (other than the how-to book or instruction manual), think about what made or makes that person you're writing about (even if it's you) who they are. What is it about their past that influenced their personalities and life choices? How do they relate to others? What are their mannerisms, speech patterns, good and bad traits?

When I was writing about my grandmother in my collection of stories, *Confessions of a Not-So-Good Catholic Girl*, I wondered how I could get readers to really "see" her, as the person I knew growing up. I read through the first draft and knew something was missing. The woman on the page sounded like anyone's grandmother. A nice lady who took pride in her cooking, sewing, and gardening. Yes, that was a big part of who she was, but I hadn't succeeded in putting *her* on the page.

I closed my eyes and thought about her for a while and that's when I remembered. My dear sweet grandma, who in many ways was a typical grandmother, cussed. A lot. And with great chutzpah. When she got mad (usually at my grandpa for not doing something around the house) or frustrated (when her pie crust would begin to break apart as she methodically pressed her thumbs around the edge), the words that spewed out of her mouth would make even a truck driver blush. Oh, and she also liked to drink. Whiskey. The cheap stuff.

Those specific details (which I "showed" the reader by recreating a memorable scene from my childhood) set her apart from your typical matronly grandmother, making her more human, more interesting to the reader.

The distinct personality traits are what separates human beings from robots. Identify what makes the character unique and show those details, not just through description, but also action, thoughts, and dialogue—*scenes*.

If you are creating fictional characters, they should be interesting, credible characters who are not perfect. Pretend you are God. That's right. You will invent a human being that is as individual as a snowflake. Show the character's good qualities, as well as distinctive flaws. His speech patterns, as well as behavior and temperament. And how others perceive him.

For nonfiction, as in biographies or memoir, write down everything you know about these true-life characters, then show it with action and dialogue, at the appropriate time. As Stephen King says, turn them loose on the page.

The **Main Character** (MC) is also known as the protagonist, hero, heroine, or focal character. **Minor/Supporting Characters** are those who are not the main point of the story but serve an important role. They are the ones who help move the story along by interacting with the main character, and oftentimes throwing in the needed wrenches to build suspense.

A writer needs to know these characters, real or imagined, inside and out. Their birthdate, the era and place they grew up, family drama, education, their loves, hates, hopes, dreams and fears, and most important, their problems.

Here are a few suggestions on how to get your characters on the page so that readers can really "see" him or her, and that you, as the story's creator, can better know and understand that character: Ask yourself, what makes these characters unique? If fictional, write out a detailed description of who your main character (MC) and significant minor characters are. Create a detailed Q & A list, to help you understand who they truly are. Such as:

Where do they live? Where are they from? What do they look like? How old are they? What is their relationship like with their family? What do they like to eat, drink? How do they dress? What do they do for a living? What are their hobbies? What are their best, and worst, life memories? (This comes in handy when showing why a character acts a certain way). What are their likes and dislikes? What are their dreams, goals? What are they afraid of? What kind of people do they associate with? And so on.

Asking these kinds of questions will help you have a better grasp of who your characters are when it comes time to put them in the story.

Keep in mind, you might not end up using every bit of this information in your book, but you should know the character inside and out. Well enough to know how he or she would react in every situation. Which leads us to . . .

## ESTABLISH MAIN CHARACTER'S (MC) MOTIVATION

What does the character want? What are her goals and what is she doing, or not doing, to accomplish them? This should be very specific. It could be an immediate need, or one that is a lifetime goal, be it career or personal, and it needs to be within the time frame of the book. Make sure the reader *cares* about whether MC will ultimately achieve that goal. As one of my literary heroes, John Jakes, says, "Write characters that readers can root for."

Here's another worthwhile quote: *We know what a person thinks not when he tells us what he thinks, but by his actions.* – author, Isaac Bashevis Singer. This applies whether you are writing about real people or fictional characters. Sure, you'll be using some narrative to get into their thought process, but the best way to reveal character is through action and dialogue, which includes internal dialogue.

Now we come to the fun part for novelists:

## FICTIONAL CHARACTER NAMES

Did you ever meet someone whose name doesn't seem to fit them at all? It may seem cliché-ish, but when you think of a man named Mario, you're not thinking blonde hair, blue eyes. Or when you imagine a woman named Sissy, you most likely picture a petite, girlish female, rather than a tall, heavy-set woman. And what about the character's name in connection with his profession? That name should fit as well. Would you have faith in a physician named Dr. Butcher? Then again, that name could work well in a horror novel. Decide what fits.

Character names should reflect the type of story you're writing, and suit the time period. For a Western, hardy, masculine names like John, Joe, Jack, and Hank would certainly be credible, as well as fit the era. If you're writing a historical romance (generally love stories set in at least fifty or more years in the past), female names might include Mary, Jane, Grace, and Ann, all of which are age-old names. Victorian times call for names like Victoria, Elizabeth, Emily . . . you get the idea. For contemporary stories, anything goes, so choose a moniker that again, suits your character and genre.

It's important to note that the names of your book's character should be varied enough not to get the reader confused. Select names with different vowels, number of syllables, and that begin with different letters. Characters whose names begin with the same letter on the page, such as Sam/Sara/Sandy, or Linda/Leroy/Laura, or Frank/Fred/Fran, etc. are guaranteed to take away from your story. As well as names that rhyme or sound alike, such as Robby and Bobby. I recently read a book in which two leading characters had names that began with M., and another two in the same story whose names were very similar. I found myself flipping back (which is especially hard to do with an eReader) to reacquaint myself with who was who. You don't want the reader to work too hard to keep the characters straight. Because many times, they simply won't bother.

The names you choose for your characters should also fit their nationality, as well as personality. Mystery writer, Les Roberts, has a book series featuring private eye protagonist, Milan Jacovich (MY-lan YOCK-ovitich)—an ex-college football player and blue-color Slovenian who enjoys a cold beer at his neighborhood pub. Creates an image, right? Without knowing anything else about him, you can already picture the guy.

So grab a book of baby names and start browsing. These books are a wonderful resource with a list of thousands of given names. You might even want to check out the obituaries, which nowadays often include a photo. This can be helpful when it comes to choosing surnames. If a photo of the person resembles what you envision your character to be, you might want to use that name (first or last, not both) or something similar.

Names should also reflect the image you're trying to portray with these characters. Keep in mind past and current trends, pop culture. If your reading audience consists of baby boomers, you might want to steer away from names like John Boy, Archie, Elwood or Geraldine, all names from popular old TV shows and so, too engraved in pop culture, thus sparking an instant image that doesn't fit the character you want them to envision.

Consider, too, those kids you grew up with, or even how you feel about your own name. Most of us, at one time or another, hated our names, but why? That question might give you a good idea for backstory n your fiction and perhaps shed some light about a real person in memoir.

Do you need to name everyone in your story? No. The waitress or handyman who serves no great purpose in the story, needn't be named. Just those who have a place in the story, who will be speaking, interacting, or creating havoc, with the MC.

Sometimes, as you get further into the story, you may realize the name you first chose no longer suits that character. Feel free to change it. But the sooner the better. Here you'll want to use the handy "Find and Replace," located on your computer and hit 'Replace all" to make the change throughout the manuscript. One word of caution, however. This will change that name *everywhere* it is mentioned. I discovered this in my manuscript for *Peggy Sue Got Pregnant*. I changed a George to an Ed, and as I perused the second draft, I saw that the Beatles names were now "John, Paul, Ed and Ringo." Oops . . .

Lastly, don't make your characters, in particular, the MC, all too stunning in features. Even handsome and beautiful people have some kind of physical flaw. How dull it is to read even a romance when everyone is simply gorgeous. Can you say *boring*?

## DEVELOPING YOUR FICTIONAL CHARACTERS

Why does a person pick up a novel and read it? Because they want an emotional experience. They want to be taken to a place that's not as real as the one they live in. It's the author's job to keep the reader from putting that novel down. Having fascinating, credible characters who learn and grow and change will do the trick. We all want to immerse ourselves when we read a book. Good writers develop characters that readers can relate to and become emotionally involved with. Readers *want* to care if the character overcomes the problem and reaches his or her goal. They want to identify with the characters, especially the main character.

This gives readers a chance to feel like they are in another person's skin, part of the fun in reading, for sure. The reader wants to laugh or cry, be intrigued, in love, or scared to death. In short, the reader wants to *feel* something.

Check out Zodiac signs, which give great characteristics of people, and is sure to spark ideas. Reading up on these personality traits is fun and will help you capture those individual characteristics. My favorite resource for this is the book, *Linda Goodman's Sun Signs*. There is also a newer book called *Secret Language of Star Signs*, by Jane Struthers, which is quite detailed. You may also check out the Chinese Zodiac, which associates birth years to the personality traits. For example: The Year of the Horse are the years 1942, 1954, 1966, 1978, 1990, 2002. Strengths include: Popular, intelligent, attractive to the opposite sex. Weaknesses are: Often flamboyant, impatient, bad temper, etc. You can see how individual, distinct qualities can make up a true, credible character!

Here are other suggestions:

* ***Do Some Serious People-watching.*** Wherever you go, listen to, and observe, how people speak, walk, act. What makes them smile or laugh or frown.
* ***Study Photographs.*** Recapture the essence of a person by describing their facial expression, how they dress. Notice every detail about that image. Do they stand rigid, or relaxed? What about their smile, or lack of? What do you suppose they are thinking in that moment?

## WRITING ABOUT REAL CHARACTERS

Here is where you can't be as creative, but you can still describe them in a creative manner. Write down everything you know or remember about that person, including flaws. Photographs are great for showing how a person stands, their facial expressions, etc.

By all means, study good books that portray true-life characters so vividly that you feel you actually know them. My favorites when it comes to stories about real people are memoirs, especially Mary Karr's *The Liars' Club*, Jeannette Wall's *The Glass Castle,* and J. R Moehringer's *The Tender Bar*. Biographies are good models for this too. My favorites in that category are *Last Train to Memphis* by Peter Guralnick, *Jack and Jackie: Portrait of an American Marriage* by Christopher Anderson, *Amelia Earhart: A Biography* by Doris L. Rich and *The Kennedy Women* by Laurence Leamer. What are you favorites?

## WHETHER YOU'RE WRITING FICTION OR NONFICTION, KEEP THESE KEY ELEMENTS IN MIND:

* **Center Stage.** Start with action, and interaction. Put your protagonist on stage immediately. Get her moving, talking, reacting. She should be introduced on page one. Show who she is and what her problem is. How does she react to this first situation? What does she reveal to the reader about herself in this scene? It can be as simple as showing her age, her background. What is it about this event that hooks the reader?

This is why you need to know your character so well. When a big scene comes up, you know how he or she will react to that situation. This will help you write the scenes and use dialogue in a believable way.

* **Appeal to the senses** – Remember there are five: Smell, Taste, Sight, Touch, and Hearing. But there is also the "sixth" sense that you may add to the story to reveal more about the character: Intuition. Does she have it? (This often means that she's probably a good observer.) Or does she not have a clue what's going on around her? Or him.

* **Focus on the small details.** Details give readers a good picture in their minds. One of the best things about being a writer is that you can have a scene or picture in your head, and if you do it right, you can transport that image into someone else's head by your words and description! When you think of it that way, you know it's your greatest responsibility to do just that.

* **It's okay if your reader doesn't fall in love with the character—as long as he is interested and cares what happens.** The MC should be the hero in the story, but he/she doesn't have to perfect, in fact shouldn't be. There may be even something annoying about the MC, but that might make him all the more interesting. Readers need to like the MC at least a little, or they won't care what happens to him. But the human flaws are what makes the MC more credible and relatable to the reader. With the other characters, such as the antagonist, readers may experience a love/hate relationship with them, but even if evil, those characters should have some redeeming quality. I have read—or started to read—books that in my opinion had thoroughly unlikable protagonists with no useful qualities. By the second or third chapter (I give them that much), I don't want to spend any more time with them, don't care what happens to them, and stop reading. Life is too short.

**Remember This:** Fiction writers have the liberty to create their characters in any way their imaginations allow, within the realm of believability. (Even vampires and wizards need to *seem* believable). Nonfiction writers are obligated to stay true to the real person. In memoir, you need to be honest and show faults, so that readers can relate, at least somewhat, to you and your personal story.

**Writing Workshop:**

## YOUR CHARACTERS' BACK STORY: WHAT'S THEIR BAGGAGE?

All characters come to your story with a distinct past, unresolved issues. Baggage, as they say. Create a separate page, or pages, describing your characters' backstory. Determine each character's past, life experiences, emotional involvements, along with the effects of his or her decisions.

Also, while you should have a full understanding of these personal conflicts from the start, your readers often don't need to see the connections until later in the story. Keep your readers curious and anxious to find out more.

## CREATE A CHARACTER LOG

Make a grid in a log or journal and list the history, traits and habits of your characters. Document what makes the character—real or imagined—an individual. Describe their unique features, personality quirks and problems. Write out their day-to-day routines, job, hobbies, and activities. Remember that characters, and real people, are both saints and sinners, and everything in between. They have their light, and dark, sides. Get inside their souls. Are they pessimistic or optimistic? Are they easy-going or short-tempered? How do they view their personal world?

Write down not just physical traits, but those details of their distinct personalities and past history. What happened in the man's past that drives him today? Why does this woman have a chip on her shoulder? What traits make him loveable, or hateful? What does she *want* in life? Why can't she *get* it?

## YOUR CHARACTER LOG CONTENTS

The following is an abbreviated example of what your log might look like:

| NAME | Main Character MC | Secondary Character | Minor Character with Role | Problem/Conflict |
|---|---|---|---|---|
| **Sex/age/birthplace Ethnicity Facial Features, hair, height, weight, body type, sense of style** <br><br> **Speech Pattern, Personality Quirks, Education, Occupation** | | | | |
| **Motivation/Goals Why?** | | | | |
| **Relationships, Past Present** | | | | |
| **Biggest Flaw** | | | | |
| **Soft Spot (weakness)** | | | | |

And so on . . .

Do the same for your antagonist and supporting characters. And, of course, with real characters in your memoir or biography. Write it all out on the chart and keep it handy to refer to often. This will help you stay consistent in your story.

Your character log could include telling details such as these, for example:

**Main Character - Name/ Role: Tony Vecchio**

**Facial Features**: Big brown eyes, goatee, his thick black hair is cut uneven, like he chopped it himself one drunken night.

**Cultural Background (i.e.: ethnicity, race, socioeconomic status, gender, language, religion, geographical area the character grew up in)**: Male Irish-Catholic, Italian from a little town outside Chicago.

**Speech Pattern:** Heavy Jersey accent, talks with a lisp

**Clothing and How He Wears It**. Wears tailored dress pants, linen or silk shirts. Yet never wears ties (the reason comes out later in book). And always wears his shirts hanging outside his pants, in contrast to the expense of such clothing.

**Make a List of Character's Likes and Dislikes**: And why.

**Add the Spices**: Distinct mannerisms. Flaws. Hopes. Fears.

**Now**: Write out the decisions he has made that brought him to where he is today, his motivations, problems, etc.

**Here is a great example of character description weaved into a scene from the book, *Sutton*, by J.R. Moehringer:** "He looks up, adjusts his large scuffed eyeglasses, the bridge mended many times with Scotch tape. Two guards, side by side, the left one fat and soft and pale, as if made from Crisco, the right one tall and scrawny and with a birthmark like a penny on his right cheek."

Can't you just picture these guys? This is from the first page of the book and certainly entices you to read further. As you read other books, pay attention to these kinds of details, which will make you more aware of how to create a credible—and interesting—character.

## CHAPTER OVERVIEW

Remember this quote by author Sara Sheridan. *"The telling of any character is what they do in a different situation."* That is precisely how you show their uniqueness. Their defined personality.

**Characters in Fiction:** Make characters believable in thought, word, and action. Make them have flaws, make bad decisions. Remember, no one is perfect and neither should your characters be.

**Nonfiction, Memoir:** Convey true-life character and experiences in ways that bring your story to life. Shine a light on your characters in a way that engages readers, and makes them feel emotion towards you, your characters, and the predicament. Ask yourself, what is my purpose for telling this story? You should have good reason and how you tell it will make all the difference.

**Try this Writing Exercise:**

**For Fiction:** Your main character is in a restaurant when there is a loud crash and a scream. What is happening? How does your MC react? Does she flee the scene, stay and help, or make things worse. Why does she act this way? On a separate sheet, make note of her past behavior that affects her present behavior.

**For Nonfiction:** Keep in mind this real person is also a "character." Describe a scene he has told you about, or that you have witnessed and write it as fiction, using the elements of fiction: Plot, Setting, Point of View, and Dialogue. Rather than the author "telling" it in narrative, bring this true story to life as if in a movie or play.

**For Memoir:** Describe a person you were close to as a child by way of a dramatic scene, with dialogue. No Narration. *Show* readers that character's personality, thoughts and motivations through action.

*Chapter 4*

# THE LONG TREK: PLOTTING & PACING

*"Plot is no more than footprints left in the snow after your characters have run by on their way to incredible destinations."*

*- Ray Bradbury*

Whether it's footprints or road tracks, plot is *movement*. It's the road the characters take, or the road not taken. It's what happens along the way, what's happened in the past, and what is yet to happen. Plot is the journey, the destination, and the arrival. It is story structure.

Whether you are writing fiction or memoir, you'll be organizing the story from start to finish. Where is your character headed? And why? What happens along the way that keeps him from his destination? Who is on the trip with him?

Plotting is the answer to these questions: **Who? What? When? Where? Why? How?** (As explained in Chapter 3 and repeated in Chapter 4.) And the key words are: **Motivation. Desires. Stakes. Roadblocks. Destination. Arrival.**

After reading the last chapter and charting their bios, you already know your characters, their motivation and desires. Now you must get them into trouble. The key words above will keep you focused on the story structure and lead you from the first page to the ultimate arrival, the last page. With all the crazy roadblocks and detours along the way.

And let's not forget setting. Where the action is, as they say.

## PLOTTER OR PANTSER?

You've probably heard the terms before. Plotters outline their story before beginning the actual writing of it. This can be a loose outline, just getting an idea on what's troubling the character and where you want the story to go. Or it could be more defined, as in a mystery, where you need to strategically draft out the main problem, how it's to be solved, and where to place the red herrings—the misleading clues to avert readers' attention from the matter at hand in order to create suspense.

A Pantser, on the other hand, is writing "by the seat of your pants." Taking a vague idea or character and seeing what happens as you write. Some writers feel that outlining is too stringent and takes away from the creative process. They like the unexpected turns that occur as they write, letting the characters lead the way into the unknown. This method can bring astute surprises for both the author and reader, and develop more creative storylines.

But it can also lead you through a tunnel that, once you see the light and emerge from that exciting journey, find yourself in a strange land, with no idea where you go from there. For new authors, I believe, it's a risk because it may cause you to have to rewrite everything you've done in the first draft in order for the story to make sense. Then again, it may make it a much improved, more exciting story. Sometimes it is worth the risk.

With memoir, you can do both. Plot out the main storyline, what you want to convey to readers about your life and the characters in it. *And* let your memories run wild. Jotting them all down as they come to you and see how it all plays out. With this art form, you do want to keep notes on these recollections and watch how the story develops.

A wonderful thing happens when writing memoir: Once you start the actual writing of the story with all the people involved, those little memory doors in your brain fly open and you begin recalling events and things that you haven't thought of in years! It will happen so much (oftentimes when you're not at the keyboard so make sure you jot it down or record it right away) that you'll actually get goosebumps remembering these occurrences that will make your story better. This is one of those golden moments of being a writer.

Being a plotter or a pantser is less of a decision and more of a personality trait. You are either a person who, when anticipating a trip, use a GPS faithfully. Or you're a true renegade who loves to just get in the car and drive where the road takes you.

Some first-time authors feel more confident doing it the way their literary heroes do it. But that doesn't always help—not if it doesn't coincide with what feels normal for that particular author. Every writer must do it the way that works best for him or her.

For example:

Nora Roberts is a pantser. She claims she never knows where her story is going until she's actually writing it.

Pulitzer-prize winning writer, Katherine Anne Porter, was a plotter, saying if she didn't know the ending of her story first, she'd never begin it.

Stephen King says, "Plot is, I think, the good writer's last resort, and the dullard's first choice." In other words, a stupid choice for dull, inexperienced writers.

A little harsh, don't cha think, Stephen?

Far be it from me to argue with The Master, but I myself could never write "by the seat of my pants." It would leave me feeling naked in the middle of a long highway going nowhere.

So I use the same approach as renowned author, John Irving, who says. "Know the story—as much of the story as you can possibly know, if not the whole story—before you commit yourself to the first paragraph . . . If you don't know the story before you begin the story, what kind of a storyteller are you?"

This all goes to show just how individual this plot vs. pants thing is. Neither is wrong. It's whatever works and what is right for you, the writer, the creator.

*However*, if you are a pantser, you will still need to jot down *some* story details (I suspect Stephen King does at least that) so you know a bit about the character, the problem and the setting.

If you are a plotter, best realize, and accept, that your original plot/outline, can change, and most likely will. And that's okay. Listen to your writer's intuition and if something adds to the story—a scene, a new character—even if you hadn't planned it that way, go with it. Whatever makes the story better. That is your ultimate goal.

## OTHER CONSIDERATIONS IN YOUR STORY'S PLOT DECIDING POINT OF VIEW

Who is telling this story? You as narrator, as in memoir? The protagonist? An unseen omniscient voice? This decision is imperative to your story and determines its tone. You also have to decide if this story will be best told through first or third person.

Yes, second person is an option, but not a great one. At least not for most of us. Mary Karr wrote her second memoir, *Cherry*, in second person, and it works because she understood the need for that POV in that particular story. When I asked her at a conference why she chose second person for that book, she explained that it's how she viewed the story, from further away, because as a teenager, that's how we tend to view the world, and that's how we look back on those years as an adult, from another universe away. Through her brilliant writing, Karr brought readers into the mindset of a young person and hooked them into the story, even from an emotional distance. The reader feels involved, and *cares*—always the key.

Karr pulled it off, but in general, reading an entire book in second person is challenging because, at the hands of a less experienced writer, the reader will most likely feel the distance and therefore, not feel emotionally involved.

So let's stick with first and third person in this chapter.

## FIRST PERSON NARRATIVE

If you are writing memoir, you will of course be using first-person, as in "I" did this, "I" felt that, but be careful with those "I's," as they can be easily over-used. Think of ways to narrate without using too many I's, to avoid sounding repetitious and thus, detract readers from your story.

Relating the story through first-person brings the reader right into the narrator's mind. It's effective when you want the reader to feel more intimate with the character, more inside his head. In fiction, a good example of first-person point of view is Herman Melville's *Moby Dick*. With the first sentence, "Call me, Ishmael," we know who will be telling the story throughout the book. Or, for a more current example, in the prologue of *The Paris Wife*. "One of the best things about Paris was coming back after we'd gone away." Here, the protagonist is talking directly to us.

But first-person is limiting. It prohibits any other point of view in the story. Readers cannot know what other characters are thinking or feeling because we can only see things through that one character's internal lens. It's an effective method when we want to see everything through that single point of view—even if it's not through the Main Character's, as in *The Great Gatsby*, where we "see" the story through Nick Carraway's eyes. Fitzgerald's method works for that story as it allows us to view the characters and their actions as if we're seeing it all through a vast picture window.

Keep in mind: When writing in first-person, you must stay consistent with the language, the "voice" used, throughout the telling of the story. And the narrator must be present, always.

## THIRD PERSON NARRATIVE

Third person is writing from the omniscient point of view. This approach allows the writer greater freedom of expression. The story can be told from more than one point of view, which often helps advance the story. But how do you do that without "head-hopping" (bouncing from one character's head to another), which could confuse the reader? You can either use a space break, put the POV character's name at the head of a chapter, or in the first paragraph of the chapter. Any way you can let the reader know immediately whose viewpoint they'll be getting.

In my novel, *Scoundrels & Dreamers,* I use third person so I can switch characters' POV, which I do several times throughout the book, though my protagonist's viewpoint is featured the most, as it should. I begin the book with the MC, Charlee Campbell. When a new character's POV comes in to play, I identify her immediately to avoid confusing the reader. How? I use space breaks or begin a new chapter with that character. For example, the third chapter opens with my MC, and I let readers know this right away with the first sentence: "Charlee didn't wait for the hospital to release her." The next chapter, the POV shifts to the antagonist, and I identify her, too, in the first sentence: "Sandra never imagined it would be so hard."

Study different books to see how the author handles point of view and first and third person. You might want to experiment and see which seems best to tell your story. You'll notice that some authors always stick to one form or another, while others switch it up. When I had the opportunity to chat with Jacquelyn Mitchard, I asked why she uses first person in some of her novels, third person in others. Doesn't she prefer one method to another? She replied that each book warrants whatever approach is most suitable to that story. Makes sense, doesn't it?

## SETTING

Now we come to where your story takes place. The sense of place. This is not just the geographical location, but also the era in which it takes place, the environment, ambience, social situation . . . as well as the time of day, and the weather. Don't forget the character's work setting, too, if it applies. What job doesn't have its share of conflict—with the boss, co-workers, or the work itself?

Setting is a vital part of the story, helping set mood, atmosphere, and impact. It's the Vibe, you might call it. Like when you travel and stop in a new town, you get a distinct feel for your surroundings, good, bad or indifferent.

By all means, don't let your reader feel indifference. Good description is necessary, of course, but in order to get readers involved deeper in the setting, appeal to those senses mentioned in Chapter 4: Sight, Smell, Taste, Touch, and Hearing. This will make readers *feel* like they are there. The right setting, executed in the right way, can make that happen.

## STORY STRUCTURE/PACING

After the first few chapters, ask yourself, how is the story moving along? Is the story problem well established? Is there enough going on to keep reader interested? This applies, of course, to whatever kind of story you are writing. Before you get too far into the plot, take time to evaluate when to slow down the action (usually through narrative), and when to amp it up (through dialogue and scenes).

Keep the story arc in mind as you write each chapter, or better yet, draw up a clear and concise "structure map" so you can refer to it often as your book progresses, allowing you stay on the right track.

Here is a simple example. It's called the Freytag's Pyramid, which symbolizes his theory of dramatic structure.

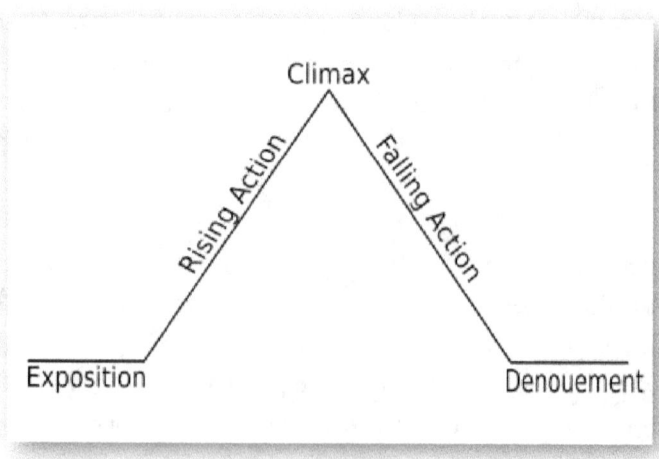

Your structure map can look a variety of ways, have varied tags, and you can find more examples on the Internet. Use any way that helps you visualize how your story is to be developed, making sure it begins with the **Hook/Inciting Incident**, moving toward the **Rising Action/Crisis Points** that builds to the **Story Climax**, and winds down to the **Resolution/Denouement** that leads to **The End.** Again, this could be for fiction or nonfiction, as in memoir.

## CHAPTER BY CHAPTER

As you write each chapter, pay particular attention to your opening line and conclusion. With each chapter opening, use a compelling lead, and end it with some kind of cliffhanger—which can be mild or mind-blowing. The key is to start out interesting and show constant progression. There needn't always be explosions or other extreme, dramatic scene at each beginning or end. It could be as simple as a conversation between characters, but one that has a consequence or moves the story further into the conflict—internal as well as external. You want the reader grabbing your book every chance they can to read "what happens next!"

As you structure your chapters, keep in mind how the MC's problems are accelerating, keeping him from what he wants. This is the heart of the story. Also, the roles of the secondary characters and those minor ones must serve a purpose. They should appear at the proper time to best keep the book's running pace.

We all know in fiction that the protagonist should not get what she ultimately wants or needs until the end, so you'll be throwing road kill into many scenes to obstruct the path and keep the protagonist from achieving her goal or reaching her dream destination.

## A WORD ON FLASHBACKS, BACKSTORY, FORESHADOWING

Both flashbacks, backstory, and foreshadowing are great tools for developing the plot. **Flashbacks** stop the main storyline by inserting a scene that gives the reader a vision of something that occurred in the past. **Backstory** injects narrative information that the reader needs to know about, but shouldn't halt the flow of the story. **Foreshadowing** adds dramatic tension to a story by hinting at what might happen next. It's the "promise of conflict," to create suspense.

While these literary devices serve a valuable purpose, they must be handled in the right way. If misused, you could confuse the reader or distract too much from the story. One way to use these techniques and avoid reader confusion is to use a space break to denote the shift from present to past and begin with a phrase, something like this: "I watched Steve approach the microphone and my mind drifted back to the last time I saw him, three years ago. When he'd told me to pack my bags and leave."

The more good books you read, the more you'll recognize how an author uses these mechanisms in their works to further their plot and benefit their story.

## ABOUT WRITING MEMOIR

There is a fine line in memoir between a life story and a self-help book and you have to decide which one yours will be. Sometimes a book can start out as a memoir but through the writing of it, become a self-help book. That's fine, just be clear on its category in order to market it correctly. Readers don't want to be misled as to what kind of book they can expect.

The basic differences between memoir and self-help is that memoir is a personal account of one's life that does not offer advice. Self-help is just as it sounds, a book that offers advice or guidance on an issue that the writer has dealt with and survived. If you're unsure of whether your book is more memoir than self-help, read several of each kind and you'll be able to recognize the difference.

## CHAPTER SUMMARY

Plot is all about decisions: Whether to use first or third person point of view. How to use the sense of place to help readers visualize your story. How and when to slow down the pace or speed it up. And how to draft your story arc.

Remember: Plot is movement and should keep the story propelling forward to the end.

**Writing Exercise:**

**For Fiction:** Not sure if you should tell your story in first person or third? Try this: Write your whole first chapter in first person. Then rewrite it in third. This exercise should clearly show which works best for you and your story.

**For Nonfiction:** Even if you are profiling a real person, that person has a story which involves a plot, and events. Those fictional story elements; conflict, setting, and point of view apply to your book as well. Glean an event or circumstance from your outline and write a scene as if you were writing it as fiction. This is a good exercise to train yourself how to tell this story in an entertaining, enlightening way.

**For Memoir:** Think of a turning point in your life and how it relates to the theme of your book. Relate the incident to a trusted friend or recount it into a recording device. The way you tell your story out loud will reveal your emotion about the event, and capture your true "voice."

*Chapter 5*

## SNEAKIN' SALLY THROUGH THE ALLEY: FIRST 50 PAGES

*"First, find out what your hero wants, then just follow him!"*
*– Ray Bradbury*

**N**ow that you've developed your characters (real or imagined), sketched out your plot, chosen your POV, and decided if you are a plotter or a pantser, it's time to get started in earnest.

The first fifty pages are often what the agent, editor, or publisher will request once he or she expresses interest in your book. These pages will determine whether they will ask for more, accept, or reject, your book. So clearly, it has to be good. Better yet, great.

How do you manage all that in fifty pages?

It's all about rising action. Get "Sally" (your MC) onto Page One, establish her problem, and by the end of those fifty pages, she better be in dire straits. The photograph opening this chapter illustrates characters in trouble. But is this man the woman's love interest and sneaking her through the alley to hide her from the bad guys? Or is he the antagonist who is only pretending to protect her and sneaking her into the alley for evil purposes? Either way, the story begins with something happening and the reader should feel anxiety for Sally and breathlessly anticipate What Happens Next.

As mentioned in Chapter 3, characters get us involved in the story. That's why your main character should enter the stage in that first awesome opening. By the end of the first chapter, readers should be engaged and have some idea as to what kind of person the protagonist is, what her problem is, and what stands in the way of her achieving what she wants. As you write your first fifty pages, keep in mind those story questions: Who? What? When? Where? Why? How? Those are the questions readers want an answer to.

But what if I'm writing nonfiction, you say? It's the same concept no matter what you are writing. Begin with a powerful statement or action. Grab the reader's attention immediately with that first sentence. Yes, I said *sentence*.

## THE START OF SOMETHING GOOD

Here are some examples of first sentences from fiction, nonfiction, and memoir authors:

In one of my favorite novels, *Open House,* Elizabeth Berg begins with this: "You know before you know, of course." Know what? How do you know? Ah, yes, you just *have* to read further.

In her memoir, *Not That Kind of Girl*, Lena Dunham opens with "I am twenty years old and I hate myself." While it isn't much of a surprise for a young girl to "hate" herself, that declaration lures the reader into the story because they want to know more. They want to know *why* she hates herself.

From the nonfiction book, *Seabiscuit* by Laura Hillenbrand: "Charles Howard had the feel of a gigantic onrushing machine: You had to either climb on or leap out of the way." Now there's a description of a larger-than-life personality! And a good opening for a book about the owner of a racehorse that became legend.

Reading such examples, I, too, wanted the first sentences of my books to bolt out of the gate like a winning horse. But a good beginning takes much thought, and it doesn't always come to you right away. So don't let finding that perfect opening sentence prevent you from moving forward with the book. (Though I realize it's a fine excuse to keep from writing, you procrastinators you.) Many times that opening gem doesn't come until you're halfway through, or sometimes not until you're done with the book.

That's what happened with my first novel, *Peggy Sue Got Pregnant.* I knew there was a better opening than the one I had. One night (great thoughts often come in the middle of the night so keep that pad of paper nearby) it entered my brain. The first sentence in that book became "It wasn't about sex." Which, of course, is contrary to the title and precisely what entices the reader to keep reading.

For my first nonfiction book, *Rock 'n' Roll and the Cleveland Connection*, I began with a statement that takes readers back to the roots of rock and roll: "In the early fifties, when rock was in its embryonic stage, Cleveland was considered one of the hottest radio markets in the country." This gives readers information many might not know and encourages them to read on and find out why.

Lena Dunham's memoir begins when she's in her twenties, causing readers to reflect on their own young adulthood, triggering their memories, which memoirs tend to do. In *Confessions of a Not-So-Good Catholic Girl*, I open with "When I was five I almost drowned."

You can see how just one opening line can snag reader interest, but then you have to follow through on the promise that this book of yours is an enticing read.

In the First Fifty Pages.

So let's go there. What are the elements that keep reader interest, be it fiction or nonfiction?

1) HAVE INTERESTING CHARACTERS
2) SHOW ACTION AND PURPOSE
3) CREATE EMOTION
4) TAKE READERS ON A ROLLER COASTER RIDE

**I Repeat:**

*C*HARACTERS
*A*CTION
*P*URPOSE
*E*MOTION
*R*IDE

You can remember this by the first letters: CAPER. Your story should be an adventure. Both in the writing of it and the reading of it.

Being aware of these important ingredients as you write will keep you invested in the story, as you hope the reader will be. And you're not off the hook once you've established that grand opening. You have to do it again, and again, *and again* with each chapter throughout the book.

One thing you might want to avoid is beginning with dialogue. Some writers think that starting with people talking will hook the reader right away, but in fact it often does the opposite. Readers don't yet know who the characters are, so they can't be emotionally invested. It might even cause confusion, or indifference, and generally not the best way to begin a story.

There are, of course, rare exceptions. Liane Moriarty's novel, *The Last Anniversary* very short, one page first chapter begins with "Do you really think we can get away with it?" This question in dialogue prompts readers to ask right away, get away with what? The subsequent discussion between two characters is lively and intriguing and it works. But again, it probably isn't the best way to begin your first book.

Now let's talk chapters. Your first fifty pages will most likely contain several chapters, especially in fiction when chapter length is often short, usually between five and twelve pages in your manuscript.

## CHAPTER MIDDLES

The middle of the chapters must move the developing story in a fluid manner. It's the *flow of the prose*. Even if you've never heard the term, you have seen how it works on the page. But it's probably the hardest to describe. Still, you always recognize it—sentences flowing smoothly, one to another. A natural progression of rhythm. The magic often is: Varied Sentence Length. You want a good mix of short and long sentences, fragments, and conjunctions, so the piece seems conversational. A speech pattern with a distinct "voice."

**Voice**. That's another part of writing we recognize, but find difficult to explain. Yet, it's actually quite simple. It's how the narrator speaks to the reader. It's point of view. It's personality. It's "listen to me tell you a story."

For the most part, it comes down to whether the reader wants to spend time with that Voice throughout the book. It can't be stilted, or boring, or unlikeable. Remember what I mentioned in Chapter One. Those old die-hard rules—never using fragments or conjunctions, or never ending sentences with a preposition—need not apply.

Make it a story you can't wait to tell to a friend. That friend is your reader. Here's a good example from Elizabeth Berg, whose voice is like listening to a friend:

From *Open House*: "I dress to bring in the morning paper. The new me. I once read that Martha Stewart never wears a bathrobe. Not that

I like Martha Stewart, nobody likes Martha Stewart. I don't think even Martha Stewart likes Martha Stewart. Which actually makes me like her. But anyway, maybe she's onto something."

And this, from Amy Tan's *The Opposite of Fate*:

"Around my fifteenth birthday, I truly became a bad girl. My foray into wickedness began with some low-grade sins. I started reading forbidden books, including *Catcher in the Rye*, which I had to buy twice because Christian family friends confiscated it from me."

Notice the cadence of both paragraphs. The *tempo, rhythm* . . . it sounds like the narrator is chatting with you. Both those examples are in first person. So what about Voice in third person? If done right, this can sound equally conversational.

From *The Story Hour* by Thrity Umrigar: "She'd decided that they were to be only friends. That Sudhir was gay or asexual or that she was simply not his type . . . So when he told her, in his casual way, that a bunch of his friends were going to hear Bruce Springsteen and they had an extra ticket and would she like to come, she almost said no."

Although these are fiction examples, you can see how the flowing prose with the right voice can mirror a memoir. When writing memoir, tell the story as if you're sitting with your best friend and relating your most intimate secrets, or greatest fear, or compelling problem, or what happened yesterday.

Here's a good example of revealing a childhood memory in *All Over but the Shoutin'* by Rick Bragg.

"I know that a few weeks later he whirled through our house in a drunken rage, and as always our momma just absorbed it, placing herself like a wall between her husband and sons. I know that later my brother Sam and I lay in the dark safety of our bedroom and tried to figure out a way to kill a grown man, before he hurt her any more."

That's narrative voice. That's flow. That's powerful. And it comes just a few pages into the book, and places you right there, in that bedroom with those little boys.

Even with other types of nonfiction, you'll want to sound like you are having a conversation with the reader. When you narrate information, refrain from sounding preachy or too authoritative, or you'll turn your reader off.

Below is an example from *Rock 'n' Roll and the Cleveland Connection*, which, despite it being basically a "history book," does not sound too scholarly, preachy or dull:

"All Clevelanders needed to hear was that there was the remote possibility that a rock and roll hall of fame and museum could be built in their own backyard. All it took was a national newspaper like *USA Today* to test their enthusiasm when it produced a poll asking about the appropriate place for a rock hall. All it took was the tenacity that makes this city's die-hard fans so true-blue . . . and ten long, agonizing, years of working and waiting and hoping and believing."

Voice. Flow. And something else. It's called the "rule of three"—a literary technique where you repeat yourself (as I did above, beginning each sentence with "All . . .") for emphasis. It's a progression, group of words, used one after another to accentuate an idea, or give your prose rhythm. Boom, boom, boom. And while you shouldn't overuse it (actually don't overuse anything), this method helps readers stay with you, as if in a dance. Left, right, left . . .

## DRAMA DRAMA DRAMA!

Of course when you are talking about getting readers emotionally involved, or at the very least, interested, there should be some kind of "fuss." This is true in both fiction and memoir. You have to raise stakes, create problems and suspense. Whereas the first chapter must introduce the character, establish the story problem, and end that chapter with a tease, your subsequent chapters should be conveying action, drama, *Oh Hell!* moments.

I could, once again, show you some good examples (and isn't it fun to be aware of great books to read?), but instead I'm going to tell you to find them yourself. Take five of your favorite books and mark what's happens from page one on up to page 80 (Because the first fifty pages in a manuscript can extend to eighty or so in a book). As you peruse your chosen books, you'll most likely find interesting things going on that push boundaries and move the story deeper, whether it's internal or external problems and situations.

In *Peggy Sue Got Pregnant,* the antagonist first appears not in person but in a letter, which enhances the suspense. In *Scoundrels & Dreamers,* we have the antagonist not only appear in Chapter One, but we get to know the woman through her own POV in subsequent chapters.

In Patti Smith's bestselling memoir, *Just Kids,* we experience the tight bond between her and photographer, Robert Mapplethorpe, and their struggles as artists. We find out in the first sentence (*"I was asleep when he died."*) that Robert's death, as much as his life, is important to the story—*and* we know up front that he will die. The emotional impact of that first sentence pulls readers in and makes us pay close attention to what happens in these "kids" lives.

Your readers should be taken for a ride where they don't know where they're going and feel anxious, or at least care, about what's to come. They want to cry, or laugh, wonder and anticipate what's going to happen next. Keep that roller coaster cranking up the track in those first fifty pages—and beyond.

By page fifty, the reader should know the who, what, when, where, and maybe even the why. And what's at stake. But they should also be hooked to the story by the *How.* How is it going to be resolved? That's the string that pulls readers into the story and ultimately ties it all together in the end.

## CHAPTER LENGTH

As mentioned earlier, your first fifty pages will probably extend through at least four or more chapters. Today's publishers tend to want shorter chapters, especially in fiction and memoir. Nonfiction works often have longer chapters. Whatever the case, be consistent. Book chapters should be about the same length. Having one chapter that is six pages, and another twenty, throws readers off, makes the book seem disjointed, and interrupts the flow of the book. Of course, every chapter doesn't have to be exactly the same length but it should be relatively close. This is important, especially with today's eReaders. Most people want to know if they are coming close to the chapter end and many of those devices don't tell you what page you're on. So with a relatively equal amount of chapter pages, readers can sense when they're getting closer to a chapter's end.

Don't forget to vary your sentence length for desired effects. **_Short for action. Longer for description._** When you want to increase tension in your scenes, use snappy, shorter sentences, paragraphs, even fragments. The reader will be right there with you. Snap. Crackle. Pop! OH NO! Use longer, flowing sentences and paragraphs to slow down the pace, or narrate some information, or when you want the reader to get inside a character's thought process, their stream of consciousness.

## CHAPTER ENDINGS

Chapter endings are just as important as their beginnings. The last paragraph of a chapter should not only bring closure to that chapter, but also lure readers to read on. You don't want the reader to stop, set your book down, and allow a chance for them to be distracted by another book, which might lead them to perhaps never finishing yours at all. Now that's a true horror story if I ever heard one.

You want to tease your reader, entice him into turning the pages. How? Throw in a tantalizing cliffhanger. Again, it needn't be loud and dramatic, but something that makes the reader say, Oh wow, I have to keep reading!

In fiction and memoir, some conflict (physical or psychological) should be introduced by the end of Chapter One. And yes, often for nonfiction, too. The reader should be well engrossed in wanting more information, then more, and more.

## WHO CARES?

Whatever story you are writing, the reader wants to feel connected. You've no doubt read somewhere along the way that a story should be *universal* in order for the reader to relate. Meaning that, even if the reader has never experienced anything like the protagonist, she wants to be able to relate or identify with the characters (even if they are vastly different from her) and the situation, or at least be able to understand the characters' motivations and the dilemmas. Readers want to feel connected to the story.

Bottom line is always, *Who Cares?*

By page fifty—or really, by page five—the reader had better give a damn.

## Writing Exercise

**For Fiction:** Describe your first love. Not just physical traits, but what did you see in him or her? What *didn't* you see . . . until much later? How did he or she make you feel? Use that memory for one of your dramatic or romantic scenes.

**For Memoir:** Do the same exercise as above, or describe your childhood home, family, or neighbors, or neighborhood. Remember emotion is the key to hooking the reader. Oftentimes what you write about your childhood or first love brings out emotions that you can use with greater clarity in your memoir. How you reflect back to a memory tells you its importance to the story.

**For Nonfiction other than Memoir:** If you are writing a how-to book, you will most likely be needing to do additional research for more information than what you already know. If you are working on a history or biography, you will definitely be doing research and conducting interviews with experts and other sources. As you work on your first fifty pages, have certain days in which you will do nothing but research. This always comes before doing the interviews. Gathering as much material as you can about your interview subject makes for a better, more defined and interesting interview. You'll gain respect with that person because you won't be asking simple questions anyone can glean from the Internet. Make it more a conversation than a formal, stilted Q & A. **Your writing exercise should include preparing for those interviews—jotting down notes and questions and securing interview dates.**

**Chapter Overview**: Have intriguing chapter beginnings and endings. Consider Voice. Alternate sentence, paragraph and chapter length. Be consistent. Remember, too, that Voice has a lot to do with using active, vivid, verbs to color the prose, like a coloring book.

*Chapter 6*

# DEAD SKUNK IN THE MIDDLE OF THE ROAD: OBSTACLES

*"The Writer Shakes Up the Familiar Scene, and as
if by magic, we see a new meaning in it."*

*- Anais Nin*

Now that you've rocked your first fifty pages, somewhere along the road, you are bound to come across a big ol' stinkin' skunk in the middle of the highway to your destination and forces you to slam on the brakes. I hate to tell you this when you are making headway and feeling pretty pumped, but . . . the above sentence is practically a guarantee.

Welcome to the dreaded, but inevitable, varmint in the middle of your book.

No matter what you write, there will be a point when you find yourself in a quandary during the process of our writing project. This is not about writer's block. It's about writing yourself into a corner and not knowing how to get out. It's about getting to the middle of your book, then beginning to question the entire work. It's a nasty, nagging little devil on your shoulder shaking his head, telling you that something's wrong, it's not as good as what was in your head.

Middles can be the worst. You would think that's when you are totally immersed in the book and things start coming together. Not always. Like that skunk in the road, somewhere along the way, you'll come upon an obstacle and you'll have to figure a way around it. Not easy when there's ongoing traffic, say, a stream of scenes that are misplaced, and in your way of plot progression. Things like that. Above all, you want to avoid the stench. Those passages you once thought brilliant that now seem to, well, stink.

Sometimes it's a problem with your characters. The made-up ones have become "real" and refuse to cooperate, according to your initial plan. Or the real people that need to be included in your nonfiction book refuse an interview, or have invented, you discover, a few things about their lives to make themselves look better, or someone else, worse. And it's why you must research and conducting as many interviews as possible. To get to the truth, as much as possible.

The problem might also be the plot. You find your original story plan is just not working. Now you must alter the entire course in order to reach a satisfying, and best, story ending. Decisions, decisions.

You have come to the part of the book that will try your patience as a writer. This is where the going gets tough. The middle of the manuscript, what I call the trenches, is when the doubt sets in. When you start to question if this book is really as good as you first thought. That maybe you should scratch it and begin a new, different, better book (like my friend in Chapter 2). That maybe you're not the great writer you thought you were . . . and so on.

This is when you ask yourself, why? Why is this happening *now*, just as you were building pages, gaining speed, picking up interesting hitchhikers?

Why? Because it must. Because books tend to take on their own life and veer off in a different direction than you may have originally planned. Even if you're a pantser—probably *especially* if you're a pantser—you now see your book through a different lens, a reader's lens, and you see it changing. You can see where the story is heading and recognize that the original plot isn't good enough for an entire book, or that something is lacking, or your life story isn't all that unique (gasp!), or your nonfiction book just isn't all that interesting anymore.

And oftentimes, it's because of those damn hitchhikers. They have hopped on board and changed the other character's life, the book's life. In nonfiction, too, some characters you didn't know about have come aboard, changing the contents of the book. Those unforeseen hitchhikers have now become essential to the story you want to tell, and that makes things a bit more challenging.

So now what?

Not to worry, I, the author who has traveled this road many times, has your back. This anxiety you're experiencing is completely normal. We've all been there. It's all part of the process. Which is to say, you are now a real bona fide, full-fledged writer. Congratulations!

At this point, you *should* question whether readers will really care about this book. And you *should* wonder if this book is really going to sell, gain a readership.

Your book has now matured. It has grown from being just an idea, a murky concept in your mind, to a real live thing—with personality. Clearly, changes must be made.

I know the trenches all too well. I was a year into my first book, *Rock and Roll and the Cleveland Connection*, when I started having heart palpations, literally and figuratively. I'd lie in bed at night thinking how way over my head I was. My heart would start pounding as dark thoughts invaded my sleepy brain. What was I thinking? Back when I believed I had this great idea? Did I actually think I could write a book documenting the vast history of rock music in a large metropolitan area when there was so much to know, so many people to interview, so many stories that had to be told? Was I nuts?

I stayed awake many nights going through all the research, all the people I still needed to talk to, as I learned more and more about my subject. Yep, I had gotten myself into some deep do-do.

But did I give up? No way. My big idea was too good. So if I didn't know how to execute it, I would make myself *learn* how. That's why when I teach my classes, I often change that common adage, "Write What You Know" to "Write What You *Want* to Know." That is just as true. And oftentimes much more interesting.

Now is the time to ask the tough questions. If fiction, what is happening to the characters in terms of development/growth and what needs to happen to keep readers hooked? (And you thought you only needed to hook them in the beginning, silly writer). If nonfiction, what other sources can I include to give the book more credibility and/or appeal? If memoir, what is the theme of this book and why am I telling it?

Chances are this book of yours, with all your doubts and hard questions, can most likely be saved, and improve with changes, but you need to look at the material as it is now, on the page, not how you originally envisioned the book.

First, deep breath. It's going to be okay. Know that you will get through this somehow, you just don't know the how yet. Get off the highway, take a break. If you continue to stare at the manuscript, you'll only get more anxious. Get away from it, by means of a vacation, staycation, or just a few days without looking at it.

But not for too long. You can even combine the break: A little bit of freedom from the book, along with time to enhance it with fresh eyes and a renewed perspective. That's where a writers' retreat, or weekend or week-long conference, comes in handy. And highly recommended. When you are in the trenches, you need to know how to get out of it. Many times, it is other writers who can pull you from that ditch. They are your source of camaraderie, moral support, and can often be of great assistance. Whether you realize it or not, these other writers are the ones who best understand what you're going through and can help you immensely. The vitality and fellowship a conference or writers' retreat has to offer is priceless.

Once you've rested up, or gotten re-energized with that shot in the literary arm at a writers' event, it's time to take a printed copy and read it out loud, chapter by chapter, as if you don't know the story at all. Try to imagine yourself a stranger, sitting in a library, dentist office, whatever, and are picking it up for the first time. At this point you aren't looking to edit the piece (that comes after this first draft, and later in this book), but to see if your story is interesting enough, exciting enough, motivating enough.

## WHAT TO LOOK FOR

Remember, at this point, you are looking for unwanted varmints that are in the way of your story, with no purpose. And because those fictional characters or real people are the nucleus of the story, you want them to have a specific purpose, and appear authentic. Do they speak and act like humans beings, not robots? Are they people you/readers will want to spend time with in a book, even if they're the bad guys? Is your main character riddled with enough problems?

Is the conflict playing out and keeping the story moving? Take a highlighter and mark all the passages where the MC is present. Is there enough action going on, or are you merely telling a story to the reader, rather than having him/her actively engaged?

And how's that plot going for you? Is it moving along smoothly, or is like that dead skunk stopping the reader? Highlight those passages where you spot places your storyline veers off the road.

## SHOW AND TELL

Notice above that it reads, show *and* tell. I'm sure, you've heard that oft-repeated phrase "Show Don't Tell!" In fact, there are some great writers who preach to aspiring writers to *never* tell—*Ever*! I disagree. Most every author must do some telling somewhere in their story. If you "show" every little incident, the book becomes a stream of scenes with no down time to allow for, say, a bit of internal conflict where the character is wrestling with his own mind, or doing some reflection. It can get exhausting if all there is, is action, action, action, all the time. We can't get inside the character's head that way.

Like author Neil Gaiman says, "Show what you need to show, tell what you need to tell." It's really as simple as that.

***Showing*** is the best way to engage the reader. It puts the reader right there in the story, in the action, gets them emotionally involved.

***Telling*** is needed at times, too. When you want to briefly describe something, or provide needed information. Such as letting the reader know a character's age or background or something about his family.

Even Ernest Hemingway does it. So does *The Master*, Stephen King. Study their works and you'll begin to notice *when* and *how* they do it, which is all-important. You will notice that although they do some telling, it's *the way* they tell that appears like showing. Again, learn by reading—and studying—the great ones.

There are always important bits of information the reader needs to know that doesn't warrant a scene. Details you want them to know about without making it into a three-act play. On the other hand, too much narrative can be off-putting to the reader. In fiction and memoir (which should *read* like fiction), readers don't want hunks of long passages with long descriptions, which can be a turn off. Just the appearance on the page, especially with no paragraphing, makes one think they're in for a long, drawn-out preachy lecture (and sometimes they are). Agents and publishers want a lot of "white space" in a manuscript—breaks that separate the prose. That's where the dialogue and action come in.

The thing is to show ***more than*** tell. You want a nice, smooth balance. A lot of scenes/action, with dialogue, and a smattering of narrative.

That said, you can get away with more narrative in nonfiction because much of it is providing information. Yet you still want to pepper it amply with showing—using quotes from interesting sources.

## MAKE A SCENE

Experiment with various ways of show and tell, or try turning some of those passages into active scenes. Especially in memoir, it's all too easy to tell the reader how you felt about something, or go on and on about what happened, without letting the reader "see" and "feel" what happened. Work on blending both the telling and the showing by using sensory images so readers can **see, smell, taste, touch, and hear** throughout the story.

Having learned these methods by reading good memoirs, I became aware of the necessity of the fine use of show and tell and made sure to dance that dance in my own memoir collection.

Here is how I told one story in *Confessions of a Not-So-Good Catholic Girl*. It's a scene from when I asked my grandfather a "sex" question (edited below for brevity). I began by *telling*. We were watching a daytime TV game show together that featured the bosomy actress, Jayne Mansfield, who the host had called "sexy." I merged dialogue with narrative. I've italicized the narrative here to clarify the difference.

"What's sexy mean, Grandpa?" *I was ten at the time and knew a lot of words because reading was my favorite activity, but this was a new one to me.*

*While I waited for an answer, I noticed Grandpa grinning, but he didn't respond right away. I could tell he was giving this some serious thought and it occurred to me that maybe I shouldn't have asked. His silence increased my curiosity, so I anticipated the answer all the more.*

Finally. "It means attractive to the opposite sex," he said, *trying to hold in a laugh, I could tell. . . .*

Now, had I simply *showed* this scene, it would read like this:

"What's sexy mean, Grandpa?"
"It means attractive to the opposite sex," he said.

That certainly robs the entire scene, doesn't it? Of personality. Of voice. Of humor. The reader misses out on the thought process of an inquisitive ten-year-old. Plus, the telling of the age itself is essential here and could only be told in narrative because the characters on stage already know the age.

So: Show with dialogue, tell with narrative.

Also: In first-person fiction and memoir, steer away from an abundant use of "I." As in "I" did this, "I" thought that, "I" wondered about, "I" pondered it, "I" . . . The oft-repeated "I" can get repetitious in long bouts of narrative. I've seen too many memoirs that use "I" when they could have used other ways of expression and scene building. One memoir I began to read—and never finished— had a total of twenty-four "I"s on one page. I counted. I put it down. If that author would've turned some of those "I"s into an intriguing scene or written it in a different way, the story would've been much more engaging. Learn how to do this by reading memoirs from established authors.

## YOUR SUBPLOTS

For fiction and memoir, another element to look for when you're in the trenches is how the subplots are working. Or perhaps, not working.

The subplots are the smaller plots throughout the book. The underlings of what's going on, including inside the Main Character's mind (his inner demons), as well as other problems. What is she experiencing besides the main conflict? Perhaps it's a complex relationship she has with a friend, sibling, parent, or coworker that is increasing her anxiety.

The purpose in having subplots—and you need to have at least one—is to intensify the drama and build up the story. The other characters besides the MC should have their own problems. And those problems should help move the story along, add more tension, and address other conflicts.

In my novel, *Peggy Sue Got Pregnant,* one of my central subplots is the relationship between Peggy Sue and her best friend, Libby. As the story moves forward, we experience Libby's struggle with an abusive marriage and her unwillingness to get out of it, which affects the bond between her and Peggy Sue, and makes life more complicated for Peggy Sue, whose main conflict is already giving her enough trouble.

Take a look at your subplots—which should be layered throughout the story—and see which ones have the greatest effect, the most useful purpose. The ones that make life more difficult for the MC. The ones that don't? Best delete.

Well, maybe not delete completely. After all, sometimes we write wonderful stuff. Passages and scenes that are just *so* good! I get that. So, if you are in love with a particular subplot, but now realize in your heart of hearts that it doesn't serve this particular book, you can always save it somewhere else. Place it in a separate file. You never know, it just might fit perfectly into another story.

Make good use of the "Cut" and "Paste" tool that is a godsend for writers. "Cut" those passages and paragraphs that don't work and "Paste" them into a different file. You can also use cut and paste to rearrange some scenes or change up the sequence of events. Placing the right scenes in the right places is essential for smoothing out the story structure or amping up the pacing.

## TIME TO DRIVE ON

Once you've done all of the aforementioned, it's time to keep going. You may notice, despite the improved changes and tweaks, that it's still not perfect, but don't get too bogged down with it at this point. You've swerved around the obstacles, at least some of them, and now it's time to keep traveling. This is only the first draft. You'll have plenty of time to go over the complete work again to make it better. Further down the road, in Chapters 8 and 9, you'll be working on the editing, revising, and slashing, so you need not get too hung up right now on making everything perfect. Save all that for the next couple of drafts.

The important thing is to recognize what needs more work, tweak what's obvious, then keep writing, moving the story forward.

*Important Note*: At this point in your book, you should have someone knowledgeable to read what you have and make constructive comments. That means **another writer** (preferably in your genre, who can point out construction flaws), an **avid reader** of books in your genre (they'll recognize when a scene or chapter isn't working), and a **trusted writers' group** (who can point out grammar and other issues). More on that in Chapters 8 and 9.

**Writing Exercise**
Besides going through and working out some kinks in what you have so far, there are a few other things to do while you are here, in the middle of the road.

**Nonfiction**:
If you are writing nonfiction, don't get so caught up with your research that you forget to write. If you're like me, it's easy to do. I love researching my topics and it can keep me occupied for hours, if not days! In the four years I worked on *Rock 'n' Roll and the Cleveland Connection*, I had a specific schedule I adhered to faithfully in order to get everything done and it helped me keep moving forward.

Make a **Weekly Schedule** that includes a specific day to do your research, whether online or in the library or museum, another specific day to do your interviews (by phone or in person), then of course, specific days to do nothing but write, and fill in those blanks granted through your research and interviews.

**Fiction**:
Same thing applies to fiction as well, because you do need to research the era that your book is set in, along with dozens of other things you need to know to get your fiction right. So novelists, too, need to make a **Weekly Schedule** for the days to work on character's bios, a day to work on the plot, a day to research whatever is needed to make the story right. And of course a day to just write!

## GO AWAY!

If at all possible, send yourself away. A few days at a cabin in the woods, lovely B&B or even a hotel down the street with just you and your manuscript is the best prescription for the dreaded middles. We all have bad habits at home that keep us from staying focused in our writing. It may because you find yourself stopping to fold laundry or do dishes or other house or yard work during your self-appointed writing time. Or you have too easy access to the Internet, allowing you to stop and check on something for your book (yes, that's needed, but not when you're facing obstacles). Or you find yourself spending way too much time on Facebook or Twitter to see what your friends are up to.

I can relate. I have these problems, too, along with my added conundrums: two cats and two dogs (please don't judge) and a retired husband. That's precisely why, when I'm working on a book, I try and go away at least twice during that time. Once when I'm in the trenches, and again when I'm doing revisions and need to concentrate, stay focused on the story. Those are important times when you need to hone in and be in the book's zone without day-to-day interruptions.

**Added Suggestion:** When you're at these places, you usually need the hotel or B&B's password to get onto the Internet. Don't get the password. At least not when you first get there. Spend that first full day writing. If you can be outside on a beautiful day, that certainly is the best scenario. After that, still wait to get online—after you've worked enough to feel that you've made true headway. My retreat habit is this: I wake at 6 a.m., get coffee, and immediately go to work. I'll break for breakfast, get right back to work, then again for a short lunch and work until dinner. I don't go online for any reason until that evening, just to check my mail for important messages.

In addition, I often take a walk after lunch and think about what I've written. Many times I'll get an idea that I can add to the book, which I do as soon as I return. The passage may be for a different chapter than the one I'm working on, but I want to make sure it gets in there while it's fresh in my mind. If I simply jot it down "for later," it can easily get lost/forgotten.

Even those times when I'm eating, I often do so in front of my laptop, or take some printed copies to wherever I am eating, to read over as I munch away. In other words, that time away is all about my book. Nothing else.

So there you have it. Besides honing a precise weekly schedule, your writing exercise for this chapter is to get invested in this book. Take yourself away, if only for a day. Maybe just to a park, or library and work steady on your book and nothing else.

Now Go.

*Chapter 7*

# THE FINAL DESTINATION: ENDINGS

*"Great is the art of beginning, but greater is the art of ending."*
*– Henry Wadsworth Longfellow*

Now that you've conquered the obstacles and muddied through the trenches, hopefully you feel more confident and secure in knowing that you really are going to reach your destination and complete this book. Yes, you can do it!

It's a great feeling to know where your story is heading and anticipate getting to that finish line and typing "The End."

But you're not there yet.

You've got some loose ends to tie up, now don't you?

If it's fiction, make sure the MC is finally getting what he or she wants, or needs. And those supportive characters, how are their stories wrapping up? Are they close to their demise, because their job is done, or have they faded from the story because they no longer serve a purpose? If they have faded, you need to explain where they went, even if it's only mentioned in a brief sentence or two.

For instance, say one of your minor characters, Suzy, had a purpose in the beginning, but no longer matters to the rest of the story. Readers still want to know what became of her. You can have her experience an untimely death, or move to Alaska, or the MC can mention to someone how she never hears from Suzy anymore. Any of those will be enough to satisfy readers. In fact, the open-ended wrap-ups can be beneficial if you're writing a sequel, allowing Suzy to pop up again. Unless she's dead. Even so, it's not entirely impossible for a character to "come back from the dead." Soap operas do that all the time and if you're writing paranormal or sci fi, it might work.

In the world of fiction, anything is possible—as long as it's *believable for that genre.* You have to be true to the type of book you're writing. Such as, in romance, the main character and the love of her life must end up together and all problems resolved.

Remember those cliffhangers you were mindful to use in your chapter endings? Use one now toward the climax that gives off a real bang, a surprising twist, or at least a startle. You want your readers' hearts to pound as they make their way to the end. This doesn't have to be an explosion, it could be something internal that causes a change in the character or plot. Bottom line, if the ending is exciting, or unexpected, or thought provoking, and concludes in a satisfying way, your reader will buy your next book. And the next. This first book is where you build your fan base.

Make sure that you have tied up all the loose ends. All reader questions must be answered by the end of the story, and in a believable way for that story. The ending doesn't always have to be happy (unless it's a romance), but it does have to be satisfying. In other words, you may know early on that a character will be dying of cancer at or near the end, but there should be some kind of resolution that makes the reader accept that fact. Or, if a relationship doesn't pan out, you don't want the reader to throw your book across the room because Jack and Kathy parted ways. Have the parting at least understandable, or unavoidable, if not happy.

In nonfiction, there are a number of ways to end the book. Have you given the reader all the info they expected to learn as they began reading the story? Have you revealed some surprising details at the end? Readers love to be pleasantly surprised and learn something they didn't expect to learn about "what really happened."

Whether it's fiction or nonfiction, the finale must be acceptable to the reader. We don't all get happy endings, but oftentimes it's when we don't get them that we learn something from that experience. Readers can certainly relate to, and accept, that truth.

So now you ask, how do I do that? How can I write endings that leave readers satisfied?

There are no steadfast black-and-white rules for how to end a book. Fiction writers have the luxury of choosing the end (or sometimes the characters choose it for you). For nonfiction, it's more complex. Know how and when to end. Follow your gut. Decide what will make the reader feel satisfied having read the book. Sometimes real stories don't always end happily, yet you don't want the reader to feel too sad or melancholy at the closing of the book. If it is indeed a sad ending, most readers want to feel some kind of hope or redemption. In the case of memoir, you can show resilience and/or show a sign of hope, or offer ideas, or provide information on how the reader, if experiencing a similar situation, can conquer their past.

Studying other books similar to yours is a great idea, no matter the genre. I suggest collecting your favorite endings and learn from them. Look at how the author weaved in all points that led to the conclusion, and how the last paragraph gives readers a sense of finality and satisfaction.

I don't want to be a story spoiler, but I do want to show you a few examples of great endings, so I'll use some well-known classic endings in fiction:

*The Great Gatsby:*

"Gatsby believed in the green light, the orgastic future that year by year recedes before us. It eluded us then, but that's no matter—tomorrow we will run faster, stretch out our arms farther. . . . And one fine morning—So we beat on, boats against the current, borne back ceaselessly into the past."

Not a happy ending to be sure, but one that leaves you with a thought-provoking image.

*The Sun Also Rises:*

"Oh Jake," Brett said. "we could have had such a damned good time together."

Ahead was a mounted policeman in khaki directing traffic. He raised his baton. The car slowed suddenly pressing Brett against me.

"Yes," I said. "Isn't it pretty to think so?"

This book ends with a memorable quote, and on a reflective note, which can also work well in nonfiction.

*To Kill a Mockingbird:*

"He turned out the light and went into Jem's room. He would be there all night, and he would be there when Jem waked up in the morning."

This ending mimics the switching out of the light the narrator refers to. Also, note that the word "waked" is used rather than "woke," which is more familiar to our ears. I believe Harper Lee chose the former because that is how the MC, this narrator, talks, and so, fits his internal dialogue.

*Love Story:*

"Not knowing why, I repeated what I had long ago learned from the beautiful girl now dead.

"Love means never having to say you're sorry."

And then I did what I had never done in his presence, much less in his arms. I cried."

This pop culture classic with the tragic ending, leaves you with an emotional moment we can all relate to, and *feel*. And we accept this ending because we knew all along that Jenny would die.

The following are some concrete guidelines to assist you in writing endings that give readers the satisfaction they are looking for and can help you gain faithful fans.

## EFFECTIVE ENDINGS IN FICTION

The MC and secondary characters should do something that causes a satisfying conclusion. This means there shouldn't be a sense of happenstance or coincidence. For example, although weather can be a component to bringing about a resolution to the story conflict, it shouldn't seem like serendipity. Most readers can tell when the ending is forced and that can disappoint, or even anger, those who have followed your story to the end only to experience a rather anticlimactic finish. They'll feel cheated and won't forgive or forget.

Having the characters resolve the conflict rather than having things resolved for them will show character growth. As you've read before, the MC should indeed evolve through the course of the book. Setting, too, can also bring about a change.

Along with avoiding all-too-convenient endings, you'll want to take note not to wrap things up too abruptly. Have you ever read a book that, towards the end, it seemed blatantly obvious the author was just plain tired of the story and anxious to get it done and move on? I know I have. You'll want to make sure those last few chapters tug at the reader's emotions, be it through suspense, surprise, or character fulfillment. In order to do that, you want to pull the reader along at a steady pace as the story progresses to its ultimate conclusion. Readers want to experience every moment, along with the character.

## TYING UP SUBPLOTS AND LOOSE ENDS IN FICTION

Some minor events are simple to wrap up, but can be easily overlooked in the grand scope of the book. For example, if a character lights a cigarette in Chapter 5, make sure he snuffed it out sometime before moving on (unless it causes a fire, which sparks another turn of events). Or if the lady leaves to go to the restroom that she comes out before the end of the book!

The subplots, those secondary storylines that added spice to your novel, need to be concluded through some kind of resolution in the end. Their conflicts, too, must be resolved in some manner.

For mysteries, you might find that you didn't put in enough red herrings or clues throughout the book to elevate suspense, or for the ending to make sense. Once you know how the story will end, you can go back to earlier chapters and add hints or bits of information leading up to it so when the reader gets to the last chapter, there are no questions left in her mind.

As you go through and tie up the loose ends, remember two essential fundamentals:

1). Check to see if the character has truly changed and experienced some kind of transformation. This could be subtle (MC learns that love is more important than material possessions) or a huge evolution that creates a surprise ending.

2) As you read in Chapter 4 on plotting, the climax is not the END of the story. Next comes the "afterplay" to bring everything to a satisfying conclusion. Remember there is the *Falling Action* that allows readers to find out what happened after the Big Event. It leads reader to the *Denouement*, the final wrap up. This is why the climax usually doesn't happen in the last chapter but one or two chapters before that, to allow for the final wrap up. And so, the last chapter is generally shorter than the rest.

## EFFECTIVE ENDINGS IN NONFICTION

How you end a story in nonfiction, as opposed to fiction, is similar in that it must tie up loose ends, and conclude on a satisfying note to the reader. The difference is, of course, that you cannot make the ending up. You are stuck with what really happened. Then again, there are a million ways you can tell the ending of that story.

For a history book, it often ends with that final year, or scene, or fact. In *Rock 'n' Roll and the Cleveland Connection*, I initially planned to do just that. End with the grand opening of the Rock and Roll Hall of Fame and Museum. However, after accumulating a lot of fun, entertaining anecdotes in my years of interviewing hundreds of musicians, promoters and fans, I decided to end the book on an even higher note: people's memories.

If yours is a book about a tragedy, you might not be able to end on a happy note, but it should still be satisfying to the reader. Again, you are dealing with truth, so there might not be a happy ending. Still, there can be a sense of hope, resilience, a moment of completion and moving on. For example, if you are writing a biography on someone who died a tragic death, you might want the book to focus on the good of that person's life, and the ending can be a reflection of his or her accomplishments, or a final good deed that person did.

You can also bookend the story. Show a final scene, resolution, or awakening from a problem or conflict that opened the book. I mentioned in Chapter 5 that in my memoir collection, I begin with "When I was five I almost drowned." In the epilogue, I tell how I faced my fear of water and overcame my anxiety by taking swimming lessons.

Perhaps the greatest example of showing victory, of sorts, at the end of a tragic tale is the story of the three women in Cleveland who were kept captive, beaten and raped for years, and emerged triumphant. Their book titles say it all: *Hope* by Amanda Berry and Gina DeJesus, and *Finding Me* by Michelle Knight. Even with such a horrific story, readers want an ending that makes them feel gratified. They do not want to feel hopeless or sad at the end of your book.

## DO YOU NEED AN EPILOGUE?

Epilogues are used in both fiction and nonfiction, but oftentimes aren't necessary in either. Some agents and editors don't care for prologues or epilogues. They find them superfluous and unnecessary, so be mindful of that. I had both a prologue and an epilogue in the original copy of my first book (the 624 page rock book). The editor kept the prologue, but decided the epilogue wasn't needed. Though I really liked what I wrote, after I did the last read-through before it was published, I had to agree with her. It didn't add anything to an already substantial tome.

The epilogue should add something to the story ending, perhaps a final surprise, consequence, or twist. While there are no hard-and-fast rules on using an epilogue, there are a few things to consider. First, if you are bound and determined to include an epilogue, keep it short. When readers are at the final pages of a book, they are ready to complete it and don't want to be dragged through a stream of passages that don't add anything new to the story.

If including one in fiction, you'll want to fast-forward the timeline between the last chapter and the epilogue. For example, if the last chapter ends in 1979, you'll want to set your epilogue at least some months later, and perhaps with a different setting, to give readers an added revelation to the MC's full story.

In nonfiction, you'll want to add a last bit of surprise or compelling twist to the story. Don't repeat anything already mentioned in the last few chapters of the book. Ask yourself if the book is stronger as a result of the epilogue. If not, delete.

## FINAL THOUGHT ON FINAL CHAPTERS

**Emotion**. That's what you want to bring to the table in the beginning, middle and end of your book. Even with a self-help or how-to book, you want the reader to feel something. Be it hope or excitement or fulfillment after reading the book. In fiction, readers want to care what happens to the characters in the end. In a series, they want to feel anticipation of what will happen in the next adventure.

Without some kind of emotion, the reader won't feel invested in the book and that will mean you have lost your readership, perhaps forever.

Remember way back when you started your book? How you made sure there was a hook to pull the reader in, get him emotionally involved in the story right away? The ending is just as important. The reader needs to care about the characters, the situation, the conflict. Now bring it all to a close by keeping emotion in the mix. It may even exhibit a range of emotions, too.

The last emotion you want readers to feel is up to you and your story. Here is a good list of the basic human emotions that can be peppered throughout your book:

**Joy/Happiness**
**Fear**
**Anger**
**Sadness**
**Hate**
**Surprise**
**Disgust**
**Anticipation**
**Pride**
**Envy**

*\*It really is all about emotion.*

## A NOTE ON TITLES & SUBTITLES:

If you haven't already conceived that perfect title, now's the time to do it. By the book's end, you know what the major theme is, and chances are there is a part somewhere in the book that reflects the overall story. This is yet another big plus about having writer friends. If you are stuck, ask them for any ideas. Many times one of them will come up with the perfect one.

**Writing Exercise**

**Fiction:**

Now that you know what you need to do to complete this book, experiment a little to find the perfect way to get the greatest emotional impact through your ending. Try writing a different version of the end. Think about the delivery. How, and when, things happen. And don't forget to add some great scenes on the way to the finish line! Remember: Reader Satisfaction.

**Nonfiction**:

If you're writing a nonfiction book, write an article on your subject matter and try and get it published. This can be beneficial in getting your name out there before the book's published, and serve you well for early marketing purposes. After all, your name will be connected to your topic.

For the book's ending, see if you can finish with a great quote from one of your sources, or a final concluding sentence that leaves reader satisfied with the overall content and tone of the book.

**The Epilogue Dilemma**: Read and study the books that have your favorite ending. How did the author do it in a way that added to the complete story? Did they use an epilogue that really packed a punch? What was it about that ending that left you feeling good, satisfied?

If you have written an epilogue, try reading that last chapter without it. Does the ending alone wrap things up sufficiently? Then maybe you don't need that epilogue after all.

If the epilogue gives the book an added dimension, a nice polished finish, keep it in.

*However*: Don't be heartbroken if an agent or editor decides not to use it. Trust that he or she knows best and accept it as part of the biz. Most times you'll realize that they were right.

# Part Two – Revise It

*"I try to leave out the parts that people skip."*
— *Elmore Leonard*

*Chapter 8*

# TROUBLE ON THE TURNPIKE: FIX IT OR DITCH IT

*"I wrote a book. It sucked. I wrote nine more books. They sucked, too. Meanwhile, I read every single thing I could find on publishing and writing, went to conferences, joined professional organizations, hooked up with fellow writers in critique groups, and didn't give up. Then I wrote one more book."*

— Beth Revis, fantasy and sci-fi author

**W**elcome to the breakdown lane. The chapter quote here reflects the writing life well. Things don't always go smooth. It's especially true once that first draft is compete and it's time to go back through it all, page by page, and revise your book. That's when you're bound to spot some trouble. It could be a stream of little things that make for a bumpy road, or huge clunkers that stop you dead in your tracks. But only the weaker, less determined, writers give up. Don't do it!

Like a broken down car, you need to find out what the problem is, fix it, or if it needs a complete overhaul, maybe start anew with something else. The important thing is to not give up on your dream if it's what you truly want. If Beth Revis can write ten books and not give up her goal to become an author, you surely can get through it too!

Now hopefully you did a little celebrating after completing the first full draft of your book. Not only do you deserve to do that, but that grand sense of accomplishment will give you a good attitude and renewed energy to dive into the *real* work.

Yes, here it comes. Revising and overhauling your manuscript will be tedious, frustrating, time-consuming, and you will bleed. Revising is total blood, sweat and tears. I realize that's a cliché, but every word of that all-too-common phrase will be your experience. You will bleed and you will sweat, at least mentally. And you will most likely cry. Because those doubts you had while in the trenches will resurface—even over the corrected parts of the book. You might see where some of those changes don't work after all, and you'll have to rewrite some pages, change some scenes.

This is your future over the next few weeks or months. Accept it and get over it.

That's my mean editor head talking. Because this is the part when you put your writer head away and bring out the stern editor head. You might be thinking right now, "Well, I'm going to get an agent or traditional book publisher and *they* will edit my book."

You would be wrong.

Sure, the agent's job is to make sure your manuscript is ready to be seen by a publisher, and that publisher will have an in-house editor (for content and marketing) and a copy editor (for grammar and line editing). But you won't get that far if the manuscript isn't already readable, well written, and well, good. These professionals aren't there to do your work. Even if they are in love with your book idea, if the manuscript needs too much overhauling, they will reject it. Or, if they do accept it, they will send it back to you to do all the needed changes. That's how it works. Don't be lazy, submit your best work!

So now you might be asking, "if I've never written a book before, how do I make it the best?" Good question. If you don't know what's wrong you can't fix it. You need to know how to recognize what's not working. Not to worry, you will see the book more clearly after some time away from it. That's why you don't look at it for a few weeks after you've completed that first draft. You're going to need a fresh perspective.

## FIX IT OR DITCH IT

When you do pull the manuscript out, begin with page one and just read. You want to take a good look under that hood and see how clean the engine is. Make sure you are in a quiet zone with no distractions during this process. As you read, be honest and critical. Rely on your intuition, which means if you stop to re-read a passage twice, chances are something's off. Take a highlighter, mark it, and keep reading. Some writers read the entire manuscript before making changes, I prefer to do it a chapter at a time. It seems less overwhelming and speeds up the process, at least for me.

You might notice some changes that you made early on no longer fit in the scheme of things, the overall story. Or that there are some things about the story arc or characterization that don't seem right, or transitions that aren't as smooth as you once thought.

Sometimes these realizations catch you by surprise. But sometimes you *knew* somewhere deep inside (that writer's intuition I've been mentioning) that something was amiss, but you didn't want to admit it so you glossed over it because it would take too much work to fix.

Did I mention being a writer is hard work?

Now's the time you must deal with the devil. Truth or Dare. If you are honest with yourself, you may find that this book didn't turn out as good as you first thought it would. Or maybe you no longer have the energy or passion to go through it all and fix what's broken. That's okay. You're allowed to ditch it. You can always start a new book. No sense investing any more time on something you've lost interest in. Many successful authors abandoned their first book, then wrote a better one and sold it. Like Beth Revis did. The good news is that all this hard labor will make you a better writer and make things a bit easier with subsequent books. So, no, that time you spent was not wasted.

If you do decide to hang in there and see this book to a polished end, good for you. That's a sign you believe in this book and feel the effort is worth it. In that case, you'll be glad you did it, for several reasons. First, every writer should know how to self-edit, it's part of being a real writer, and that's your goal, right? Second, you want to impress the professionals with your competence. This can benefit you in the future as, chances are, the agent or editor will want to work with you again because of your proficiency and attitude, and so, make your next project easier to sell. Third, you'll feel a great sense of pride at how great your book turned out. Once you are done with all the hard work, you'll have a mean, clean, gleaming machine. (Okay, cliché noted—and if you're going to use a cliché, make sure Reader knows that you know it's a cliché.)

Ready to fix it? Okay, let's do this.

## SECRETS OF SELF-EDITING

Editing one's own work takes time, patience, and know-how. It's also necessary. You want this manuscript to be as clean as you can make it before sending it out to anyone, even if you have a professional editor. Their job is hard enough and you want them to know that you're a conscientious, professional writer. You also should want to learn what to look for to improve as a writer.

Because there is so much to know and this chapter only addresses the major issues of editing and revising, I suggest getting a good book on self-editing your manuscript. I've used several over the years, a few favorites are *Revision &*

*Self-Editing, Manual for Writers & Editors,* and *Self-Editing for Fiction Writers.* There are many other good ones, too, of course.

Whichever ones you choose, have those editing books on hand after you give your book a thorough read-through. On a positive note, you will most likely find some awesome passages that will have you blushing with pride. Places where the prose flows smooth as car wax, the dialogue of the MC is dead on and interesting, or the quotes from your sources improve the book in a meaningful way, or a story in your memoir is so touching that it makes you cry. Those kind of passages make you feel like you are a real writer after all!

There may even be parts of this book of yours that are so good you feel like a damn genius! Okay, hold on. That might not be a good sign. Remember way back in Chapter One, I mentioned the term, "Kill Your Darlings?" Those are the words, sentences or paragraphs that seem *too* brilliant and often are. How can that be? What does that mean? It could be the passage is too wordy or overly descriptive, or the words too fancy, when simple ones would do. There may be too many lengthy descriptive paragraphs, or long flowy phrases that throw the story off kilter and distract the reader. While you might love what you wrote, if it doesn't serve a great purpose in your book, you need to kill it, or at least put away somewhere else, like in another book or another life.

As you begin to read it through, you might indeed discover a whole lot more wrong than you anticipated. It may not resemble the book you originally envisioned, but that doesn't mean it's a bad thing. I must say, each of my books, when completed, turned out to be much, *much* better than I ever imagined when I first envisioned them. Not only did the book become better simply by writing it (and not just dreaming it), but by going over and over it to make it a smoother, intriguing read.

First, look at the *appearance* of the pages. I find it easier to see when it's all printed out. For each book I write, I purchase a 1 ½ inch or 2-inch three-ring binder (depending how long the book is) and a paper puncher to cut the holes to fit into the binder. After every chapter, I print out the pages and place them inside, like a real book. The best part about this practice is that you see the progress made every time you complete a chapter and watch the book grow. That alone is encouraging!

The appearance should look clean and neat. Do you see an ample amount of white space on the page and a wide border of one-inch margins all around? Or does the page look crowded with few paragraph breaks, little or no dialogue? We've all read books where there is an entire page of narration, description with nothing that breaks up the prose. Those are the parts that people skip. Look to see where you can use some space breaks, especially for scene transitions and shifts in time, or location, or place, or point of view.

Basically, it should *look* like a book, except that it's double spaced, which is industry standard for manuscripts. If you find passages that seem to go on and on, tighten up the prose and look to see where you can break it up into more paragraphs.

Next, with pencil or pen, write notes on that printed page of everything you read that needs tweaking, a better word choice or phrasing, or sentences that could be better. Then, take a yellow highlighter and mark every place you made a note (easier to see on the page so you don't miss any of those notations). After each chapter, go into your document and make the changes. This is how I do it and it works great. You will find more typos and things that are wrong when reading on paper than on the computer screen.

## BOOK LENGTH

There are generally two common flaws in a completed first draft. It's either too short (less than 50,000 words) or too long (more than 120,000 words). Both can be fixed. If it's too short, think about adding more scenes that enhance the story. If it's too long, decide what doesn't enhance the story and cut. Even a great scene should be eliminated if it doesn't move the story along. Remember, you can always cut and paste anything into another file to use perhaps in another story.

## WHEN YOUR BOOK'S TOO LONG

You realized a while ago that this book was getting too long because you've seen the word count. If you are writing nonfiction and it's a historic tome, it can be pretty much as long as it needs to be. But if you're writing a novel, depending on genre (like mystery) or subgenre (like cozy mystery), the general length is between 70,000 and 100,000 words. Chances are, if your manuscript now weighs in at 120,000 or more, you've got some editing to do.

Sometimes it's just a matter of tightening up the prose here and there. This means going through each sentence and eliminating unnecessary words. Other times, there can be whole passages that need to be excluded. If you have no clue on where to go from here, or there are deeper issues, summon your astute and faithful writers group. Or maybe it's worth calling in a doctor. For your book, that is.

A professional editor for hire can help at this point, but you might want to save him or her for after you've done your changes and need a pro to do a more thorough examination. As the writer of your book, you will often recognize what's not necessary, but don't want to admit it. Now's the time to admit it.

As daunting as it may seem to have to go over and cut, cut, cut, or rearrange, at least you have something to work with, which is better than having the other problem, which is:

## WHEN YOUR BOOK'S TOO SHORT

This issue calls for more thinking, writing and creativity. For fiction, if you are at, say, 40,000 words and it's not a novella, think about adding more active scenes or another conflict, or bring in a minor character to increase story tension. For nonfiction, think of more sources you can interview, or research for more facts that can increase reader interest. Have a pow wow with your writers group and ask for some troubleshooting. Many times, your peers can bring up viewpoints and ideas you hadn't thought of.

Be careful, though. Don't add things willy nilly (now there's a fun phrase, isn't it?) merely for the sake of adding to your word count. You want to add for the sake of the story. Always remember that.

## TUNE UP TIME

Once you've cut or added to your story, it's time for fine-tuning. You may have been editing for clarity as you wrote the first draft and that's fine. For nonfiction, especially with history or a book with a lot of facts, editing as you go makes sense. You want everything in the right order, tell the story in an authoritative voice, with sources quotations and all the important information. However, you can still be creative in the telling of the story so that it doesn't read like a boring textbook, and that can be enhanced in the revision process.

For fiction, and memoir, it helps not to worry too much about editing as you get the story down. It really does fuel the creative process if you refrain from editing as you go, and let the creative mind go to town. Get it all down first, so that you have those great scenes and conflict and those tension building relationships that pepper the manuscript. When you're finished with the first draft of the book, you'll most likely be far beyond the standard word count, but you'll also have some great stuff to work with. You'll then be able to recognize the not-so-great stuff that needs to be deleted.

## PURCHASE COLORED MARKERS

Colored markers are great tools for editing. These will be used to highlight various parts of your book. Use one color to highlight the dialogue, another for narration, another for changes in POV, and another for first and last paragraphs. You'll want to mark the first sentence and paragraph of every chapter to see if each one does its job by hooking the reader's interest, and sparking curiosity of what's to come. Check the last paragraph in each chapter to see if it ends with some kind of intriguing passage to get readers anxious to move on quickly to the next chapter. We've all read reviews that say, "I couldn't put this book down." That's directly due to great chapter endings. And that is your mission.

## A CHECKLIST AS YOU EDIT

* Print out your manuscript after inserting page numbers and place in your binder.
* Check your dialogue and see if each "voice," is distinct and readers can identify the characters simply by the way they talk. You don't

want characters to sound the same. Check if every conversation helps move the story along.

* Refer to your characters' bios and ensure that individual traits remain consistent throughout the book. If your MC's eyes are blue in the beginning and brown elsewhere, you'll want to catch that before a reader does.

* Check chapter length, which should be fairly consistent. Remember, you don't want one chapter with eight pages and another with twenty-eight. While there is no "set" chapter amount, length does matter in order to keep consistent. Novel and memoir chapters tend to run shorter (generally no longer than fifteen pages), while nonfiction is often longer because it's generally information based.

* See where you can use stronger, more effective word choice, active verbs, and lively prose. Use that "Find" tool at the top of your document and see how many times you use the same word. This is often a real shocker. We all tend to reuse the same words over and over without realizing it. See where you could change some of those repeated words with a different, better, word.

* Finally, when you are done editing your second or third draft (you'll be going through this stage more than once, guaranteed), now's the time to place your beloved manuscript in another's capable hands—your Beta Reader and your genre reader. Next up in Chapter 9.

## Writing Exercise:

When rewriting, revising, and reworking, it's often best to work outside your normal writing area. Grab your laptop or hard copy and head out. To a park, coffee shop, library, or beach and start plugging away. A different environment allows you to see it all with a fresher outlook.

This truly makes a big difference. I like to save up money while I'm working on a book so when I reach this point, I can take off to a Writers' Retreat (when I need to be around writers, ask questions and share thoughts), or a hotel (when I need total solitude to work). We all need a few solid days of being nothing but a writer. When you're surrounded by beauty, new scenery, and good vibes, it allows your brain to rejuvenate, which breathes new life into your work—and your thought process.

*Chapter 9*

# SIRI, DID YOU GET THAT? READERS & EDITORS

*"Either write something worth reading or do something worth writing."*
*- Benjamin Franklin*

**H**ave your suit of armor ready? You're going to need it.

As you now know, revising and self-editing are rough roads, but necessary to complete this journey and reach your summit. You must hand over your baby to a trusted colleague, who can read it and provide insight and helpful suggestions before you send your work to agents and editors.

But before you do, be aware what the genre/subgenre of this book is, in order to pitch it correctly to an agent or publisher and market it accordingly. Ideally, you knew from the start what kind of book you are writing, but sometimes stories change as you write them. You may have started out writing a romance, but as the story evolved, it became more of a mystery, or is no longer the same book you started.

That's okay. It happens all the time. So now's the time to be clear on the type of book you have written.

With nonfiction, the genre category is, for the most part, clear-cut. There is Memoir, Creative Nonfiction, Business, Self-help, Biography, History, Reference, True Crime, among others. With fiction, it's a bit more convoluted. The most familiar fiction genres include Mystery, Romance, Women's Fiction, Science Fiction, Horror, Thriller/Suspense, Fantasy, Historical Fiction, Children, and Young Adult (often called YA), targeted for adolescents and coming-of-age groups. There is also a more recent category, New Adult, for readers in their twenties.

Once you've decided the correct genre for your book, do your homework. Find out what the rules are for that particular category. And there are rules. Such as, with Romance, there must be a "happily ever after" ending. Each genre has its own convention and obligatory scenes.

For example, here are a few basic rules for Mystery:

1) Plot is the driving force, but the sleuth, most often the MC, is just as important and must use his or her wits and skills to solve the mystery.
2) Action should begin right away and a crime committed within the first three chapters.
3) You'll need a varied list of suspects.

4) Throw in a few red herrings—false clues that point in the wrong direction to amp up suspense.

5) The end should be a bit of a surprise, with all plot points wrapped up.

Once you are clear on your book's category, you need to explore the more complex subgenres, which nowadays often overlap. What's the difference between genre and subgenre? If Romance is your genre, you need to know, based on the story, whether it belongs in the subgenre of Contemporary Romance, Christian Romance, Romantic Suspense, or something else. See what I mean? Complex. Even more so with women's fiction, which is what I write. To clarify, *Romance* is primarily focused on romantic love and must end with the two lovers, *finally*, getting together. *Women's Fiction*, which certainly can include romance, highlights women's issues of the time period in which the story takes place.

For example, my debut novel, *Peggy Sue Got Pregnant* addresses premarital sex and unplanned teenage pregnancy. This was a huge social "Scarlet Letter" problem in the 1950s, which is the era in which the book opens.

Knowing your book's distinct category will help booksellers place your book in the proper section. Granted, when the book gets shelved in a bookstore, there is usually no subgenre section, but when it comes to online promotion and marketing, you need to hone in on that readership.

## YOUR BETA READERS

Now that you've established category, you're ready to find the right person to read your book. It doesn't have to be another writer but should be someone who reads that particular genre. These are the important people in your writing life. They will be your sidekicks, your copilots . . . your "Siri." In the book biz, they are called your Beta readers.

These readers are not editors and aren't looking at your manuscript for grammatical errors, necessarily. Rather, they are people who love to read the genre of books you write. And as such, they can spot when things seem amiss in the story. They may still catch grammar and spelling errors, but their main purpose is to see what's not working in the story itself. For example, someone who reads memoir will recognize if you haven't included enough vivid detail to spark real emotion. Someone who reads mysteries will notice if there's not enough suspense or intriguing suspects. Your Beta readers will let you know if a scene doesn't work, if the story loses momentum, if the plot doesn't seem plausible, a character doesn't feel believable. Overall, they will check if the book reads smoothly from chapter to chapter, and winds up in a satisfying way.

See why you need them?

## WHERE TO FIND THESE TREASURED READERS

Here are some tips:

* If you know of no one who reads the kind of books you write, it's easy to make these friends through social media. There are many reading and writing groups all over the virtual map, but it might be best to start with the most popular—Facebook and Twitter. For example, I belong to the online group, Women Fiction Writers Association, which has thousands of members, and if needed, I know I could ask one of them to peruse my manuscript. However, if you decide to approach someone you know only online, make sure you have had a dialogue with them before, through the organization's Facebook page or their website's Forum page. Also, let them know you'd be willing to do the same for them. This is definitely a reciprocal situation.

* Belong to a group for book lovers. There are bound to be a few right in your hometown. Find them through your public library where they often announce their meetings. There are also, most likely, local online "Meet-up" book groups in your area you can find simply through Google. For example, when I type in "Northeast Ohio Book Clubs," there were two full pages filled with book clubs of a variety of interests, and the first one listed is a "Meetup" group. These are community based groups for local meetings of mutual interests and

networking. People in book groups would most likely be thrilled to read a "real" manuscript.

* Searching for Beta readers should begin well before you need them. Besides getting to know book lovers on social media, you could attend local author book signings or be involved in online launch parties. Attendees at these events are obvious fans of the genre, so chances are you'll meet like-minded souls. For example, if you're a sci-fi writer, you're bound to meet others there and can easily strike up a conversation about your favorite books. You never know who you will meet. Don't be shy about exchanging business cards or email addresses. It's always great to get to know people who share your interests!

* Although Beta readers normally are not paid, you can always buy them a cup of coffee or lunch when you meet to hand the manuscript back and forth, or do some other favor for them. They will be spending a lot of time reading and commenting, and you want to let them know you appreciate them. Be sure to thank them in your acknowledgements page. They deserve that for their time and effort, and everyone loves to see their name in a book! And just think, you'll probably now have a dedicated follower *and* guaranteed critique reader for your next book.

## HOW IT WORKS:

There are a few rules to getting your manuscript critiqued properly. First, do not hand over the first draft. Your manuscript should be in pretty good shape so your reader isn't sending time correcting things you should have caught. Also, send it to your reader in the way he or she prefers. It's easier to email it, of course, but not everyone uses an eReader. Some still prefer print, which means printing out every page of your manuscript. Yes, that's an added expense of ink and paper, but remember, they are doing this huge favor for you, so make it easy for them.

Establish what you need from them as far as comments, critique, suggestions, fact checking. The best way to do this is give them a check-off list.

Provide your reader with a detailed question-and-answer sheet. Here is a sample of the list with questions I have used for my Beta readers:

1. Did you get hooked in the story right from the first page?
2. Were the characters—real or imagined—interesting?
3. Did the fictional characters seem like real people?
4. Did the story feel believable?
5. Was it written in a way that kept your interest, or were there parts that lagged, or made you want to put it down and not pick it back up? If so, why?
6. Did you find yourself anxiously anticipating what happens next?
7. Was there any point in which you felt confused, or something seemed a bit off?

Tell your Beta Reader to be totally honest. Better to hear it now than hear it on negative reviews once your book is out in the world.

Lastly, make sure you agree on a time limit to hand it back. If you don't, you could be waiting much longer than you anticipated. A reasonable period would be six to eight weeks. You may be asking yourself, what do I do while it's in their hands? Easy answer: Write something else. If there's going to be a sequel, get started on that. Or begin a new story. The important thing is to keep busy and not allow yourself to think and wonder how your Beta Reader is doing on the book. *Do not go over your copy while it's in another's hands.* This is your break time from the manuscript, so that when you get it back, your mind will be fresh and you'll read it as if it's a new book (well, almost).

When your pages comes back, go over all the notes your reader made, and be objective about the points made. This does not mean you must change everything they mentioned. Ask yourself, "Will this make the book better?" This is where you need to be honest for the sake of your book, not your ego. At the same time, if you disagree with the reader's suggestion, you are not obligated to make the change. It's still your book, and you should always follow your instinct. Just remember to be open-minded.

## WRITERS' GROUPS

I've mentioned before about the importance of belonging to writers' groups and attending workshops, conferences, and retreats. If you have utilized this massive benefit in your writing world and taken advantage of these avenues, you can now hand-pick who you want, and trust, as a Beta Reader with your full manuscript.

If you have yet to be a part of a critique group, there's still hope. You want to seek out those who love to read and are writers, too, because they are word people and that's what you want. Here are two suggestions on how to find them:

* You can start your own writers' group by advertising at your local library or meeting other writers at conferences and writing classes.
* Find a Meetup group for writers in your area, join and go to the meetings. Some give writing prompts ahead of time to share on meeting day. Others are more free form. See what works for you.

Here's how I became a member of two writers' groups: The first one began more than twenty years ago. I learned of it through my writing teacher/mentor who had formed it. She passed away seven years later, but our core group of eight still meet once a month. The second one, with six regular members, has been meeting for almost ten years. Five of us met in a creative nonfiction class and became fast friends. Although we all wrote CN then, each of us has ultimately delved into different genres that include YA, children's, romance, women's fiction and suspense. We now also have a poet in the group.

Writers groups are invaluable in many ways. Belonging to a group of other writers forces you to write. You can't get critiqued if you have nothing to bring to the meetings. Knowing that your next meeting is just days away prompts you to sit in that chair and produce. It helps you learn how to be disciplined and make time for your writing. Best of all, you will make new friends—who often become your best friends.

## TIPS FOR A SUCCESSUL WRITERS' GROUP

Every critique group is different, with varied ways of workshopping. Some groups prefer to email their work to each other so members can read and comment before meeting day. However, that takes up quite a bit of personal time. Reading all those papers ahead of time can be difficult to do when everyone is busy with work and family obligations. Just deciding on the meeting day can sometimes be a challenge! Because of that, my groups prefer to bring our printed pages on the scheduled meeting day. We then take turns reading the pieces out loud and comment right there. We block off three to four hours meet-time and try to workshop everyone who brings something. If we run out of time, the person who didn't get critiqued is first on the list at the next meeting. This works out well for everyone.

It's good to note, too, that those pages should always be double-spaced. That's good practice right from the start, as it is publishing standard for manuscripts. It also gives everyone enough white room to make their notes and corrections. Also, your group should decide who reads the pages. It could be who wrote it, but it's also a good idea for someone else to read it. This way, you can see how an unbiased editor or reader would read it as far as voice and flow goes. Sometimes it's easier to catch something amiss when it's read by someone who didn't write it.

So how do you evaluate someone's hard-written work? Gently. "Word choice" here is as important as choosing the right ones in writing. You don't want to hurt anyone's feelings, so be sure to give constructive comments. Rather than "critique," recommend or suggest how the writer can improve the piece, from grammar to content. Always, always, include a positive remark. Be a good team player.

If you're the one getting critiqued, be open to everything that is mentioned. If more than one person agrees with said comment, it's a good idea to revisit the section and heed their suggestions.

Some of the issues that group members need to address are: Grammar mistakes (of course). Poor opening. Sentences or passages that are unclear and confusing. Awkward sentences and descriptions. Lack of smooth transitions. Poor word choice. Dull plot or characters.

There are some writers, maybe even you, who get defensive about *any* negative comment regarding about their work. This does not help one become a better writer, and isn't that the main reason writers have a critique group? Your motto here should be: Listen and Learn. You'll be surprised how your work will improve as a result.

While you should consider all the group's comments, the ultimate decision on changes is up to you. Then again, if you have a good group whose members are people who read and write every day, chances are, they are probably right.

## WORKING WITH AN EDITOR

When an editor marks up your page, don't get heated about it. His, or her, job is to make you look good. Be grateful he caught what you didn't, and make those changes.

There are times, of course, when you will disagree and immediately want to defend that passage or suggested revision. Give it a few days, then read it over again, out loud. You may be surprised to discover that the editor is right after all. *Or* not. Yes, sometimes an editor is wrong. They are human, too, don't forget.

When you see that an editor's suggested change does not enhance the story, or your research proves his/her opinion is wrong, you'll want to discuss it if you're working with the publisher's editor. I believe the best way to do this is over the phone or, if possible, in person, perhaps over coffee somewhere. Make sure you email first and you both decide on the best time to talk. Never call an editor out of the blue.

When you do have that talk, explain why you feel that passage needs to remain as is. Most times, if your reasoning is valid, the editor will comply.

## FINDING AN EDITOR

If you are not getting published with a traditional publisher, you need to find a good editor yourself, which is not always easy. You can, of course, google for a professional editor, or find them through LinkedIn. But don't forget the opportunities to meet editors at writers' conferences where you can meet them in person.

Hiring a professional is a worthwhile investment all around. Yes, that means you'll be spending money, but I promise you it can pay off. Fees vary widely. Some editors charge by the hour, others by the page, still others by the word. You can figure spending at least $700 or more to have a full manuscript edited. This all depends, of course, on the length of the manuscript, and years of the editor's experience. If you cannot afford this, start saving your money as you're writing (remember my money tip in Chapter 2) so you'll be ready when the time comes.

If you are a serious writer who wants to be proud of the book that has your name on the cover and improve your changes for good reviews and sales, you need to invest in your book. A skilled editor can save you from embarrassment and heartbreaking nasty reviews in your future.

Now, before you hire an editor, ask other authors for referrals. In addition, do your own private research on potential editors. Find a few of his clients and email them (you should be able to get authors' email addresses through their website), or private message them on Facebook. Tell them you are considering hiring that editor and politely ask about their experience working with that editor. This extra effort can save you from disappointment down the road.

So there you have it. Beta Readers, writers groups, and professional editors are your best friends in this business. They will guide you along this publishing highway, help you fill in those pot holes, and make for a smoother trip overall.

**Writing Exercise**:

Make your own **Calendar of Events** of what's happening in your writing community.

Go wherever you can meet like-minded souls. Such as:

Visit your local library and see what kind of events they offer. Do they host a monthly book club? Is there an author visit coming up? Are they offering a class for writers? Make notes in your calendar so you can attend.

When you find out about a writers' group, see if they are open to new members. Joining a group can help you become a better writer, *and* you'll make new friends who share your love of words.

Spend some time googling writer conferences and retreats. You never know what you'll find that will have you saying "I have to go to this one!" Best to find these a year in advance to ready yourself time-wise and finance-wise. Many offer Early Bird Specials to save you money. Once you find these gems—*Mark them in your calendar and go*!

# Part Three – Publish It

*"An author's strong belief and enthusiasm will affect the writing of the book and often the publisher's commitment to it."*

*- Sterling Lord, literary agent*

*Chapter 10*

# VALET PARKING OR SELF-PARK: YOUR PUBLISHING OPTIONS

*"I think you have to believe in your destiny; that you will succeed, you will meet a lot of rejection and it is not always a straight path, there will be detours—so enjoy the view."*
—Michael York

There is much you need to know and consider when it comes to publishing books. First of all, not everyone is going to make the big time, and that shouldn't be the "be all, end all" of your goal, anyway. As an aspiring author, you'll want to write a book that you are passionate about so you don't run out of gas before your destination. I don't recommend that you ever write a book for the sole purpose of becoming rich and famous. Think about the authors who have really made it big. The names come easily: Stephen King, Nora Roberts, James Patterson, Janet Evanovich, John Grisham, Dean Koontz, Danielle Steel, and let's not forget the renowned billionaire, E.L. James, author of the *50 Shades* Series. There are more, of course, but the list is relatively short compared to the millions of writers throughout the world who have written books.

Be aware of the odds. Yes, you can try and write a book that's similar to the top sellers of today, but that effort won't be enough to fuel the energy, drive and passion needed in writing an entire book because you're doing it for the wrong reason. Also, by the time you complete it, acquire an agent, or get a publisher, that trendy ship will have sailed to a remote island. Even those who have been in the book industry for years cannot predict how long a trend (remember the hot-selling vampire-themed books?) will last, nor what the next one will be.

Don't go there. Don't put all your hopes and dreams into such a small basket. Pull out the big storage bin and give yourself some room to write the best book you can, then explore the many options that are available in publishing today.

## DECISIONS, DECISIONS

When I began writing my first book, I dreamed of having an agent, getting an advance with a big publisher, and seeing my book on the bestseller list. Most authors I know have had that same dream. But even those who do achieve that high-reaching and difficult goal, the accomplishment came through in a variety of ways and are as individual as the author. Everyone's story of success is different, and every success level is different, too. You can be successful without an agent. You can be successful without a big publisher. You can be successful if you decide to self-publish. It all depends on a number of factors, many of which will be addressed in this chapter.

When it comes to publishing, there are a number of lanes you can choose, and I've gone a different route nearly every time. At this writing, I am the author of six published books, including this one. Four nonfiction, two fiction. My nonfiction books have been published by three different companies. The novels from yet another. These publishers include a university press, a national traditional publisher, a POD (Print on Demand) company, a small New York publisher, and with this one, I chose CreateSpace.

The reasons I approached these individual presses are as unique as the companies themselves. You must research for the company that publishes the kind of book you've written, or writing, and one that would serve you best. Because I did that, I've been pleased with each of the books produced, and was allowed to maintain at least some creative control in the finished product. That's one of the perks when you go it alone, or with a small press, where the staff is more likely to work hand-in-hand with you, from content decisions to art decisions. On the other hand, it's wise to consider all the publisher's suggestions and guidance because, after all, they are in the business of creating books.

The important thing is the book itself. As author, the ultimate publishing decision is yours. This is why you need to know and understand what your options are. And to do that, let's first learn the differences between traditional publishers and self-publishers, and identify the pros and cons of each.

***Remember*: Nowadays both traditional and established self-publishing companies will produce a quality product. It is up to YOU to provide a QUALITY, WELL-WRITTEN, WELL-EDITED MANUSCRIPT!**

**The Definition of a Traditional Publisher:** Professional publishers that offer the author a contract to publish their book. The company prints, publishes and makes the product available to booksellers and retailers. They do not take any money from the author, and oftentimes, will provide an advance that will be offset against future royalties.

**The Definition of a Self-Published, or Indie, Publisher:** The author publishes a book on his own, independent of a traditional publishing company. This means all responsibility is on the author.

## TRADITIONAL PUBLISHING

*Pros:*

**Credibility:**
If this book is your first, decide on what your purpose is for publishing. If it's to launch a professional career, you might want to begin with a traditional publisher. Why?

* You'll receive guidance by professionals in the business. They know about the industry and can help you achieve a professional product.
* You'll get professional advice on how to produce the best book possible.
* Your book will receive in-house editing by an experienced, professional editor.
* You'll be taken more seriously by the media, booksellers, and the industry.

**Money:**

* You won't have to pay for any of the production, the editing, or the art.
* You won't have to do your own bookkeeping on sales. You will receive your royalty statement via email or regular mail.

*Cons:*

**Time:**

* It takes time to find the right publisher or agent. Time spent drafting query letters, your novel synopsis or book proposal, and sending to

prospective agents or publishers. More time will be spent awaiting a response, which can take anywhere from a few days to a few months. Then, after receiving your share of rejection letters (accept this, it's part of being a writer), you'll send out a new batch and beginning the process over again.

## Production:

*   In Chapter 2, I mentioned the Three Ps: preparation, perseverance, and professionalism. You might want to add another one, Patience. Because you're going to need it. Production through big traditional publishers takes a long time. Your book will generally be released anywhere from 18 months to two years *after* the manuscript has been completed, submitted, and accepted. It may take a little less time with smaller presses, but then again, it might not. It all depends on the size of staff.

## Art:

*   As a general rule, the art director has complete say-so on what the cover of your book will look like, and how many photos will be included in the book. Once again, smaller presses are more open to asking authors for their ideas about photos, and also about book cover ideas.

## Marketing

*   Much of the responsibility of marketing and promotion for the book will lie with the author. Yes, even with a big traditional press.

**The Duty of Self-Publishing:** The author assumes all financial and promotional responsibility.

## SELF-PUBLISHING

_Pros:_

### Credibility:

* If you are an established professional freelance writer, or have already authored a book published by a traditional publisher, you'll often be taken more seriously as an author. This status will separate you from the pack of first-time, self-published authors. Unfortunately, in many cases, there remains a stigma related to self-pub authors, only because many produce inferior work. Best way to change that? **Publish Good Books.**

### Time:

* Whether you publish the book yourself, with a POD company, or as an eBook only, it will take nowhere near the amount of time as with a traditional publisher. Usually under four months.

### Complete Control:

* You are King or Queen of your world, _er_, book—with complete say-so on every aspect. However, with that freedom comes much responsibility.

_Cons:_

### Credibility:

* As mentioned before, self-published books often still wear a Scarlett Letter when it comes to being respected in the profession. The reasons are diverse and will be discussed later in this chapter. Your credibility will come through you, not a reputable publisher, so you will need to

have establish you're a professional platform, or brand, before your book is published.

**Money**:

* Because the author assumes all costs, it will take some time before the book will make a profit. If you going to be truly indie published, this means you must form your own company, pay for an ISBN, hire a copy editor, and cover designer. You will need to sell enough books to cover your investment. But after that, you'll receive 100% profit. If you go with a self-publishing company, you will pay others to do this for you. And you will still have to buy the printed books. If using a Print on Demand company, books are generally sold to authors at a 40% discount.

**You Are Your Own Publicist:**

* It's great to have total control. But that also means work. You must arrange book signings and speaking engagements, publicize online, alert the media, etc.. It's like having a full-time job. The more you know, and the more people you know, the easier this part will be. Just know that marketing takes time *and* money. Part Four addresses this topic in full. Realize that you're going to be very busy before, and after, your book is published!

**Want to go the Traditional Publishing route? Here are the required steps toward that goal:**

**Step 1.** Have your dynamite, professional query letter ready to go.

**Step 2.** Have your dynamite novel synopsis or book proposal ready to go.

**Step 3.** If fiction, your book must be complete before pitching agents or publishers. If nonfiction, best to have at least 1/3 of the manuscript complete.

**Step 4.** Research agents and traditional publishers (only publishers who accept unagented submissions). You can find a comprehensive list in the *Writer's Market*, an encyclopedic annual resource book for writers. Once you have a list of no less than ten names, be sure to go into their website and check their particular submissions guidelines, and follow them to "T." Their websites should give you all updated information, such as the current editor at a publishing house, and how to submit.

**Step 5.** When an agent or publisher asks for the manuscript, or sample chapters, have it ready to go. Which means, don't wait for them to ask before you revise and perfect your pages, do this before you send the queries out!

**Your Manuscript**

**Formatting:**

* Your Title Page: On top upper left corner, single-spaced, include contact information. Include genre and word count on top upper-right corner. About one-third of the way down, centered, enter your title, subtitle (if you have one) and your name, all in CAPS. Do not number this page.
* Your story starts on Page One. Manuscript should be *double-spaced*, single-sided with 1" margins on all sides. On every subsequent page, your name/title/page number must appear on top right corner of each page.
* Use the most acceptable font, Times New Roman, Point 12, unless otherwise requested by agent or publisher (usually Arial or Courier).
* Start each new chapter on its own page, with chapter number and chapter title (if there is one) in CAPS. Begin body of chapter four lines below title. Indent five spaces for each new paragraph, except the first. (Use the automatic first-line header for the indents. Do not type it each time using the space bar, or tabs. Doing so will create havoc for the typesetter.)

* Have your manuscript in pristine form before sending it off. No typos, or grammar mistakes. Have your Beta Reader, or other readers, go through before you send it anywhere. Now you are ready to submit!

**Submitting:**

* Send out a *single-spaced* professional business query letter first. Never send a manuscript without request.
* Have a list of five to ten editors, agents or publishers you want to query. Make sure to keep track of *where* and *when* you send them so you know when it's time to do a follow up.
* Always adhere to their submission guidelines, which can vary from company to company.
* Yes, send out "simultaneous submissions" with queries! Doing one at a time and waiting for a response from each would take forever, and unfair for an agent or publisher to ask this of you. That said, if they ask for an exclusive on your manuscript, by all means agree! Though make sure there's a time-frame established for a response (six to eight weeks is reasonable). More on this topic in Chapter 14.
* If sending snail mail (and only by request), include an SASE or SASP for a return reply (and hope they don't use it!). Positive responses almost always come through a phone call or email.
* Follow up! Editors are busy, busy, *busy*. Wait a reasonable amount of time (usually six weeks), then send a polite and professional email (no phone calls!) and ask if they've had time to peruse your query or manuscript. Mention your name, title, and date that you sent it.
* Keep Writing! Whether you're waiting for a response or mourning a rejection, keep your butt in the chair and work on something else, or, if you realize your manuscript wasn't up to par, start reworking it.
* Always, always, save everything on a flashdrive. It's also a good idea to email the manuscript to your inbox so you can retrieve it anytime, anywhere.

* Don't use staples if you snail-mail the book. Use paperclips, or simply leave pages loose. Remember to always have your name, book title and page number on every page.

* Don't assume the rejection is misplaced. It may well be that "It's not you, it's them," but sometimes it really is you—not personally, but professionally. You may have to rework that piece to make it salable. And that's okay. It's what writers do. If you receive a hand-written rejection with suggestions for improvement, rejoice! That means you're almost there. Rework it and send it back to that same editor.


## OFF THE BEATEN PATH: THE SELF-PUBLISHING ROUTE

Some people give up after several rejections and decide to self-publish. That is certainly a viable option, especially with so many choices today. Yet, there are many things you need to consider. First, it needs to be a good book. A really good book. That means well vetted by your writers group, professional editor, and your Beta reader before it goes to press. It amazes me that some writers will spend money to self-publish their book, yet not spend money on hiring a good editor who will make it the best it can be.

If you plan to self-publish, I plead with you:

**If you're willing to spend money to self-publish, spend some of that money for a professional editor.**

It's the best advice I can ever give. Even if you've been a schoolteacher all your life, chances are, there are bound to be things that you will miss. It's nearly impossible to catch everything—even if you make your living as an editor! That's right. Because while it may indeed be grammatically correct, there might be something about the content that needs reworking. Another set of professional eyes will often see what you don't. Once it's out in the world you'll be glad you did.

Speaking of money, you need to have quite a bit of that. The cost to self-publish print books can be anywhere from $600 to $10,000, or more.

Also, it's good to know that the most well-known self-pub companies are under the same corporate umbrella: <u>Author House</u>, <u>Xlibris</u>, <u>iUniverse</u> and <u>Trafford</u> are all imprints of <u>Author Solutions</u>, a name you'll see a lot of as you begin to research self-publishing. When you research, be sure to look for in-depth articles on the companies before making a commitment.

Also, consider the marketing angle. Big chain retailers like Barnes & Noble often won't carry your book in their stores, saving space for the traditionally published books. You'll most likely have better luck with your local indie book stores, whose owners are generally supportive of local authors. The best way to sell your self-published books will be at speaking engagements, book fairs, or other personal appearances.

Self-publishing means full responsibility. You want to make sure that your product is professional, of high quality, and have a ready-made audience. If you're writing a nonfiction book, you want to make sure there will be no legal problems in what you wrote. This is another good reason to be a part of a writing community. There is bound to be someone who knows, or knows someone, who can get you in contact with a lawyer knowledgeable about your subject matter.

Lastly, in case you're not sure what a POD is or does: This is a digital printing process that can print books as you order so you don't have to have boxes upon boxes of your books in your garage or other storage area. This is a terrific option. You order as you need, and will, in most cases, receive books within a week or so.

**Here are the required steps you'll want to take toward DIY (Do It Yourself) Publishing:**

**Step 1.** Complete the book. Revise and revise until it reads smooth and looks like a professional polished manuscript.

**Step 2.** Have a "Reader" knowledgeable about the genre of your book to read it over for anything that may be amiss in the content of the story. Then have your work vetted by a respected, professional editor. **Remember This**: You do not want to publish a book with your name on it that no one will read or buy because it's poorly written or produced.

**Step 3.** Read how other self-pub authors have done it, and gain marketing tips those sources. When possible, talk to these authors, especially those who have been successful at it, and ask about their experiences, good and bad.

**Step 4.** Once you've done a significant amount of research, decide whether you will self-publish using your own imprint (indie publishing), or go with a POD company, or publish it only as an eBook. Will this be your one and only book? If you take the eBook or POD route, there are a number of companies to choose from, and different priced packages. If you're planning multiple books, want complete control and have the money, you might consider forming your own indie company. No matter what you decide, you'll want to be informed on all matters of concern before cranking up the publishing machine.

**Step 5.** Have a budget. Costs for self-publishing vary widely, whether you do everything yourself, or pay a company to produce the book. While some options may cost little or nothing to produce a book, there are still expenses, such as for book cover art, and a good editor.

**Step 6.** As stated in Step 5, you'll want to hire a professional editor and graphic designer to produce a dynamite cover. Most companies provide these, for an additional cost, in some of their packages.

**Step 7.** If you choose to publish under your own company (imprint), register it under your state's business law, as a trade name. As stated earlier in this chapter, you must buy your own ISBN number, which I refer to as the social security number for your book. You need that number for booksellers to find your title. You'll also need to find a good printer, copyeditor. In addition, it might be a good idea to obtain an LLC (Limited Liability Company), particularly with nonfiction books, as a precaution against personal liability.

**Step 8.** Begin marketing before the book's release. Set up a book launching party, some signings at book stores and other suitable places, depending on your subject matter, and if possible, secure radio and/or TV appearances. Include those event dates in the press release, which you'll have ready to send out weeks before publication date. And of course, use Social Media to create a buzz. Just don't overdo it. If you post something about your book every day, you will lose readers before you even get them.

## ON ePUBLISHING (Digital Books)

If you would like to have your book available as an eBook only, this is yet another option. The biggest advantage of ePublishing is that you can get your book online quickly and relatively easily. Go to any of these companies' websites and they'll guide you through the process step by step. Another plus is that if you find mistakes once the book goes live, you can go back and make changes anytime, something you cannot do with print copies (at last not without added expense). For this reason, some authors decide to publish an eBook first to allow for any changes or updates, then publish in print later on. Many eBook publishers do print books as well, so you have both options open to you at any time.

When my collection of essays, *Confessions of a Not-So-Good Catholic Girl*, was complete in 2008, I was turned down by agents because memoirs by "unknowns" generally don't sell well enough unless you have a horrific, or wholly unusual, story to tell. Plus, as was told to me often, collections of stories, be it fiction or nonfiction, are usually not big sellers. So I decided to use a POD company and was quite happy with the experience. I had total control, which meant a lot to me because that book was such a personal one.

Back then, eBooks weren't all that popular yet. But soon after, eReaders became a hot item. So a few years after that book's publication, I contacted the publisher (Infinity) and they formatted that book for me and made it available within weeks. Of course there was a fee, but I didn't want to take the time to learn how to format it all myself since I was working on my next book, so it was well worth it to me. Again, everyone's needs vary.

DIY ePublishing means exactly that. You will need to format your manuscript according to publisher's instructions, and make sure any images are the right resolution. It's quite a process, and can take a bit of time, but it means that you can have your book out there in a short amount of time, and done your way.

**NOTE:** Although this chapter contains much information on self-publishing options, make sure to do additional, updated, research online. And don't just go into their website. Google the company name and see what comes up. You can find articles and other information that can be helpful in terms of their practices or other matters of concern. It's wise to subscribe to *The Independent Publishing Magazine*, which will give you the latest in what's happening in the indie world.

Below is a short list of popular eBook and print self-publishing companies, with a *brief* overview. The conversion process and the royalty details can be confusing, and there are changes constantly. So you will need to do research for the latest information, and to make the right decision for you. Again, make sure you understand everything fully before committing your book.

### AMARON KDP (Kindle Direct Publishing)

When you publish with Amazon, your book will be available on a Kindle eReader only. So that's something to consider. However, Amazon is currently the top book seller, and authors are paid up to 70 % royalties each month, more than most. In addition, the process is easy and can get your book "live" in a day or two. Note: **For those confused about KDP vs. CreateSpace**: The latter is for print books produced and sold through Amazon.

### BARNES & NOBLE NOOK PRESS (formerly PubIt!)

This method is user friendly as it allows you to upload your manuscript from most any file, including Microsoft Word, the most common, and will automatically convert to the ePub format at no cost, which is a big advantage. The disadvantage is, like Amazon KDP, your book will be available only through their Nook eReader.

## CREATESPACE

This is a good option these days to get your print book published your way. But again, the book should be well vetted, with no typos or spelling errors that can embarrass you once the book "goes live." With CreateSpace, there is no cost involved in publishing, however, it does charge the usual 40% distribution fee, and extra for services. Like most, the company offers service packages, for layout, cover design, editing, and marketing assistance. But beware that this convenience can be costly, if you're on a tight budget.

You'll notice that I've used CreateSpace for this book. Why? It benefits me more as an author for a how-to book. Also, because this is a reference, I wanted it done exactly as I envisioned it in looks and content. I wanted a book that I, as a writer, would want when seeking out knowledge, and to be best presented, with good visual content that coincides with the various topics. I did, of course, pay for all the images and cover design, but I felt it was the right route for this particular book.

## LIGHTNING SOURCE

**Lightning Source** is part of the Ingram Content Group, one of the largest distributor of physical and digital content, and so, another option for print and distribution of print-on-demand books. A few of the differences between Lightning Source and CreateSpace include: Lightning Source offers the choice of both paperback and hard cover books, whereas CreateSpace only prints paperback. There are no author services such as cover designs offered by Lightning Source, so files need to be fully designed before uploading. Createspace charges no setup fee, Lightning Source does. Again, if you plan on going this route, do your homework and see what would be a better choice for you and your book.

## SMASHWORDS

This is yet another digital publisher that is free to publish and can be uploaded from Microsoft Word files. Authors control price and can decide anytime if or when to put the title on sale to boost sales. Author royalties range from

60-80% of the list price. The advantage here is that your book can be available through several eReaders, such as Kindle, Nook, and Kobo.

## BOOK BABY

Has an upfront cost of $99 to set up your eBook. There is no commission charged, and authors are paid 100% royalty. That is, after any eBook stores take their cut. Book Baby has a wide distribution, including Kindle, Nook, Kobo, Apple, among others.

## BOOKLOCKER

Specializing in nonfiction and how-to books, the price here is also $99, though the fee raises if your book doesn't meet their detailed layout criteria, which is extensive. Royalty payments, from 50-70 %, depending on eBook price, are paid every month

## LULU

With Lulu, you can do it yourself for free, or pay $99 to have them convert your manuscript for you. Authors receive up to 90% royalties (minus e-bookstore standard take of 30%) and your eBooks will be available on several eReaders, including Apple. This company also provides services such as copyediting, designing images and cover designs for an additional fee. Be aware that once you set the price of your book on Lulu, you're stuck with it. That is, unless you withdraw the book, then you must republish it to set a new price.

## NO MATTER WHAT YOU DECIDE

I repeat: Make sure you do your homework before releasing your "baby" to any self-pub company. Check out their websites, blogs and writers' message boards to understand their criteria and what each has to offer. Also, there are informative websites and chat rooms for deeper investigation on their business practices, etc.. These include Preditors & Editors, Absolute Write Water Cooler, and Writer Beware.

The best information often comes from those who have done it. Ask several self-published authors about their experience. It's always good to get this first-hand knowledge and is another invaluable reason to attend conferences and workshops—to meet these authors.

As mentioned earlier, unless you are writing only for a small group, such as a memoir for family, or a book for a small business, try to pursue a traditional publisher. You never know how this may benefit you in the future, especially if you want to write another book.

Happy Publishing!

**Writing Workshop:**

Take a few days to do nothing but research. If you're going the DIY route, start exploring companies, as well as talk to other authors who have gone that route (at writer events and book signings). Think about your book cover and what you'd like it to look like. Check the services provided by your chosen POD company, or research other possible book designers. If you are going to have your own imprint, make a plan on hiring the right editor, and choose a reputable printer for your book. Make a list of qualified people you want to approach about writing a review for your back cover blurb (see Chapter 15). Also, begin to check requirements for book reviewers—some want an advanced reader copy four or more months before its release.

Invest in the latest edition of resource books. I recommend the *Writer's Market* and *Jeff Herman's Guide to Book Publishers, Editors and Literary Agents.* Both include an extensive list of publishing companies.

*Chapter 11*

# LOADING ZONE: CONSTRUCTING THE NONFICTION BOOK PROPOSAL

*"Now is one of the best times to be a writer. There are more
subjects to write about, more ways to promote, and profit from
books, and three billion readers on the Web alone."*
*— Michael Larsen*

This chapter and the two that follow, the novel synopsis and the query letter, are the business angle of writing your book. All three of these topics are of utmost importance if you are aiming for a traditional publisher. And even if you are planning to self-publish, you still need to be aware of them because it's part of the book world you are now in.

While this chapter focuses on nonfiction, I encourage writers of fiction to do most of the steps we'll address. Why? It will help you look at your book as a business person. It will help you think like a salesperson. And it will help you write a more focused book and be able to market it in a more successful fashion.

Although it can vary somewhat, there are nine basic parts to a standard nonfiction book proposal. As you're drafting these sections, you will likely discover things about your book that you hadn't thought about, so it's beneficial to draft it out whether you end up selling it to a traditional publisher or not.

Even if your book is fiction, you'll need to do some of these proposal elements, such as writing an overview about what the book is about, drafting a marketing plan, organizing a chapter outline (or at least story arc) and of course, completing those first few chapters to get the process moving forward.

For a nonfiction book, you need to have a concrete book proposal to begin seeking an agent or publisher. Unlike novels, and most memoir—of which agents/editors usually want to see the completed story—you do not have to have the book finished to begin pitching a work of nonfiction.

Here are the most common elements of a standard book proposal:

1) **Cover letter**
2) **Cover page**
3) **Overview**
4) **Marketing Information**
5) **Competitive Analysis**
6) **Author Info**
7) **Chapter Outline**
8) **Sample Chapters**
9) **Attachments**

Before we cover each step in greater detail, you should have two things set in place to help you maintain a solid focus on your book: A great story idea and dynamite title. You may come up with an even greater title as you write the book, but it's good to have something concrete in mind as you begin.

Start thinking like an agent, editor or book publisher. This means asking yourself, will this book sell? Will people want to read it? This is one of the reasons you want to write the proposal before you get too deep into the book. The proposal will get you looking at it as a tangible product rather than a vague idea.

You want to begin drafting a book proposal early on, before you get too far into the book. Preparing the nine steps to a book proposal will help arrange the book in an ABC way, and hone your thoughts and ideas. It will help you become a more concise writer because every word in a proposal must count. That means no unnecessary words, no awkward sentences. And nothing that's not absolutely interesting. After all, you want to get that editor or agent excited about your book.

Once your proposal package is thorough and well written, you'll know exactly how you are approaching this book, how it will develop, and how it will end. Then you'll be ready to draft a rockin' query letter, which will be your first introduction to the editor or agent. You should have the proposal ready *before* you send out your query letters because if the agent or editor responds right away (it does happen) and asks for your proposal, you'll want to have it ready to send out that day, while their interest is high. (More on the all-important query in Chapter 13)

Okay, here we go, step by step:

1. **COVER LETTER**: This is a professional business letter where you reintroduce yourself and remind the agent/editor that you are sending this proposal upon their request (as it should be). So of course, you'll be writing this after you receive the go-ahead, using the correct name and address of the agent or editor.

2. **COVER PAGE WITH THAT GREAT TITLE**: A great title grabs attention and that's precisely what you want to do. At the top left

hand corner, add your name, all contact information, including email address, single-spaced. Your title will be about a third of the way down, in the center of the page. Below that, double space, then the *By*, another double space, then your name.

3. **THE OVERVIEW**: An overview is a one-to-three page (double-spaced) detailed description of what your book is about. In well-written third person prose, state the main benefits and features of your book, who will want to read it (be specific about your audience) and why your readers will want to buy your book instead of similar titles already published. The lead paragraph should be a real attention-grabber. (For examples, read the inside cover flap on the books similar to yours.) Add a paragraph that explains why *you* are qualified to write this book, and what you'll deliver. This should be written with crisp, concise language using active verbs to describe how awesome this book will be (enthusiasm make a difference, just don't overdo it).

4. **MARKETING INFORMATION:** Nowadays, no matter who your publisher is, you, the author, is largely responsible for marketing your work, especially after the initial launching. Publishers need to be convinced that your book will sell. Think outside the box and list a few distinct, creative ways you plan to promote your book to your target audience. Mention organizations you belong to that relate to your book's topic or genre. Nonfiction authors often become known as experts on their book topic and you want to capitalize on that. How? By doing group presentations, radio/TV spots, and speaking engagements. So be sure to mention your willingness to do that. Include any syndicated columns or blogs you may have that target your proposed audience and book topic. Suggest places, other than bookstores, that you plan to market your book. For example, for my first book, I did signings at record and music stores, special musical events, and music history presentations at libraries, book clubs, and even on a rock-and-roll cruise. These are the best opportunities to sell many more books than at a bookstore. People who attend are your target

audience. They are there because they're interested in your topic. So if you do a good job, they will most likely buy your book at the end of your talk (more details in Chapter 15).

5. **COMPETITIVE ANALYSIS:** This is where you will tell the agent or editor why your book will stand out from the other titles on that topic currently available. What are those other books and how is yours different? A list of three to five is good. Feel free to mention the similar titles by the publisher you're approaching, or the books by the agent's clients. You want them to know you did your homework, are familiar with the books they've published, and then note how yours will be different. Without, of course, dissing those books. You simply want to make sure your approach/angle is different, and show that you'll be offering something the others don't—without disrespecting or putting down another book.

   *One thing you don't want to say is that there is no other book out there anywhere like yours. There may be a reason for that ;-). In other words, your book should have a readymade audience. Plus, if your book *is* similar to a bestseller—but different—all the better. Agents and editors are looking for the next big seller. That said, best stay away from "hot trends," which will most likely be gone by the time your book is published.

6. **AUTHOR INFO:** Why are you the right person to write this particular book? This is what the agent or editor wants to know. Mention, in third person, any experience that qualifies you as a leader in this topic. It could be that you've written extensively on that topic for newspapers, magazines or in your blog. Have a Master's or PH.D in the subject. Have work experience in that area. Have done in-depth research on the topic. Have unique and specialized training in that areas. Belong to an organization specializing in that topic. All of these are credible reasons why you are the right person to write this book.

   Why write this in third person? Once again, this is industry standard and makes the proposal more formal and professional.

7. **CHAPTER OUTLINE/ TABLE OF CONTENTS:** List the titles of each chapter (make them interesting!) and include, in parentheses or bullet points, specific details on what will be covered in that chapter.

8. **SAMPLE CHAPTERS**: These are completed chapters that will give the agent or editor a good idea on your writing style and how you cover the material. Most publishers request three chapters. Usually it's a good idea to include the first one, to show how the book opens, then two of the best, most compelling chapters in the book. So no, it doesn't have to be chapters 1, 2, 3. It can be 1, 5, 9 . . . or whichever ones you think can sell your book the best. However, I have seen one company specifically mention that they *do not* want the first chapter. So be sure to check their submissions guidelines and follow instructions. If they don't specify chapters, again, send your very best.

   The sample chapters should demonstrate your writing skills, subject knowledge, and exhibit your passion for the topic. As mentioned throughout this book, that first chapter should hook the reader and grab his interest. You might want to open with a startling statistic, or intriguing true story, or personal anecdote that sparks the reader's imagination. And like your entire book, each chapter should close leaving the reader wanting more.

9. **ATTACHMENTS:** These are any photographs, articles, illustrations, graphs charts that will be included in your book. The articles would be those that you have published on the subject *and/or* that cite an important source that you plan to interview for your book, or perhaps have already interviewed, which gives you instant credibility. If you don't have clips of articles you've written (and published) on the subject, try your best to make that happen. You're writing about it anyway, so see if there's a publication that can publish your article on the subject, then include it in your proposal.

**Other Details:**

* Other than the cover letter, your proposal should be double-spaced.
* Use Times New Roman, Font size 12, unless otherwise requested.
* Do not send proposal unless requested, and then send it in its entirety in an attachment.
* Begin each section of the proposal on a new page. Use bold subheads to break up text, make it clear and neat and easy to read.
* Provide your website or blog information in the body of your email.
* When all is said and done, your nonfiction book proposal will probably be somewhere between 20 to 40 pages.

That's it. Yes, it does take time, but it's a necessary part of the book business. This will be your sales tool when you are ready to get that agent or publisher.

Good Luck!

**Writing Workshop:**

Work on those three sample chapters first. This way, you'll have something to draw from when you write out your overview, chapter outline, marketing and competitive analysis. Plus, the longest part of this proposal, those chapters, will already be written.

Another suggestion: Write an article on your topic and try to get it published in a newspaper or magazine. If not, there are plenty of online publications, and don't forget blogs. This is great writing practice and you can then include the published piece in the attachments of your book proposal.

*Chapter 12*

# THE SHORT CUT: THE SUCCINCT NOVEL SYNOPSIS

*"When you start with your main character, not a news headline,
you've increased your chances I'll keep reading."*

— *Janet Reid, literary agent*

The novel synopsis is basically making a long story short. I've never been good at that. But I've done it and lived to tell about it.

Just when you think the hardest part is over—finishing the novel—you'll discover that drafting a finely tuned synopsis is like being caught alone in the woods without a compass.

Ah, but you do have this book. I will guide you by the hand and get you through this gnarly trail of snags and over brush, and back on the highway to publication. But *you* have to do the hard work. The only way to avoid it is if you are not seeking an agent or traditional publisher. But as I've said before, you should at least try that route.

I am being honest when I say I'd rather write a complete novel than write a synopsis. The challenge is telling the complete story of your 80,000+ word book in just three to five pages. So yes, it's hard, but it can also be of great benefit to you. With my first novel, I found a discrepancy in the manuscript as a result of going through the main points of the story when working on the synopsis. It was minor, but could've been embarrassing if a reader had noticed it. So that mindful tweaking alone made for a smoother read. When the book is ready to launch, you don't want any Bumps in the Road!

## THE RULES

There are distinct rules to abide by when you write a synopsis. You must adhere to a well-defined format, according to most agents and follow the standard guidelines. And the rules can often be confusing. For example, do you single space it or double space the synopsis? In her blog, Miss Snark, a literary agent, says: Synopsis are traditionally single-spaced. She adds that there should be double lines between paragraphs, no indents. And, as in the manuscript, one inch margins all around.

While most agents prefer a one or two-page, single-spaced synopsis, there are some who request three to five double-spaced pages, though usually for longer works. Always check the submission guidelines on their website. If they don't mention a preference, go with the above standard.

The first page of our novel synopsis should include author information at the top left corner, with the genre and word count directly across on the top right hand corner. The novel's title should be centered, in caps, about a third of the way down. Begin the synopsis four lines below that.

So where does your name, title and page numbers go on subsequent pages? Generally it's in the upper left-hand corner, title in caps. Like this: **Adams/ BOOK TITLE/Synopsis**, with the page number directly across to the right. If your title is more than two words, you need not put it in its entirety here. Just enough to identify yours from the hundreds of others they read. With my first novel, *Peggy Sue Got Pregnant*, I wrote it like this, **Adams/PEGGY SUE/ Synopsis.** Simple and clear.

When you first introduce the characters, use CAPS. Describe the story problem and how it develops and ends (yes, include the ending). All without going into a lot of the subplots or the minor characters.

Just the facts, ma'am.

All in just a couple of pages.

Right. I know.

## WRITING THE DREADED SYNOPSIS

Okay, here we go. Welcome to the gnarliest part of writing a novel. It's a trail full of snags and over brush in a field of tethered sticks and stones. It might not break your back but it *can* try your patience. But that's why I'm here, to help make this task easier and less complicated.

Let's define it first: The synopsis is a condensed version of your novel, providing all the key information: The Characters, Plot, Theme and Setting. The purpose of the synopsis is so the agent or editor can know what the story is about without reading the entire book. So focus on the essential parts of your story, and in chronological order. The synopsis should have the beginning, middle, and unlike the query where you don't reveal the end, you must provide it here.

In fluid prose, describe the main conflicts and plot points as they occur throughout the book. Introduce main characters and describe how their relationships evolve, or dissolve, from beginning to end. Include also the external plot (what's happening in their world) and internal plot (what's happening in their head).

Even if your book is written in first person, always use third person in your synopsis and present tense to make it more immediate.

The next page is an example. This is the first page of my own novel synopsis to give you an idea on how it should look on the page.

Deanna R. Adams
MY ADDRESS
MY CITY, ZIP
PHONE
EMAIL

Commercial Women's Fiction
Length: 110,000 words
Novel Synopsis

## SYNOPSIS: PEGGY SUE GOT PREGNANT

**Hereford, Texas, 1957:** When sixteen-year-old PEGGY SUE LAWRENCE meets nineteen-year-old FRANKIE LONDON, she has no idea this Southern boy is about to change her life forever. When Frankie arrives at her house with his parents for a Welcome-to-the-Neighborhood dinner, she's intrigued by his good manners, charm, and love of music. She and Frankie begin seeing each other on the sly, knowing her parents would forbid a romance due to their age difference. Besides, Frankie is a musician, and according to her daddy, music's not a viable trade, and most musicians are womanizers.

Now, she's pregnant. How can that be? She and Frankie only did it that one time—before he left for Nashville. Since then, he's been traveling back and forth to record, and she hasn't had a chance to tell him. Peggy Sue decides to tell her parents first. After all, Frankie doesn't need this kind of news with his career just taking off. Her parents react to her news worse than she feared. They stick her on a Greyhound bound for Cleveland where she'll stay with her mother's sister, AUNT JO, and her husband, RAY. Peggy Sue is forced to leave everything behind, including Frankie, and best friend, LIBBY MORRIS.

**Cleveland, Ohio:** On the long bus ride, Peggy Sue meets an older black girl, ANGELA HANSEN, who tells her that she regrets giving up her own child six years before, which helps clinch Peggy Sue's decision to keep her baby. When Angela gets off in Detroit, the two promise to stay in touch. Peggy Sue finally tells Aunt Jo—who can't have children of her own—that she plans to keep the baby. Her aunt tells her that the only way possible is if she and Uncle Ray adopt the child, stressing that it must remain a family secret. Peggy Sue's world is shaken further when she receives a package in the mail from someone claiming to know the truth. . . .

Notice I referenced the change of city in a heading. This eliminated the need to write it out in prose, saving the space for the story itself. Right way, the reader knows where the scenes are taking place without risking making the synopsis longer. Notice I used caps the first time I mentioned the main characters, but not after that. Also, the tone of the synopsis is similar to the tone used in the book. This is especially important since, in the story beginning, Peggy Sue is sixteen-years-old and thinks and acts as such.

Whether the agent asks for a long synopsis (three to five pages) or short (one to two pages), I suggest writing a longer version anyway. This makes it much easier to get everything you think needs to be in there before you start worrying about tightening it up. In the first draft, don't be concerned about length, just condense the novel's story best you can. In the subsequent drafts (and there will be several), you'll cut and tweak as necessary. Once you think it's as good as you can make it, print it out and put it away for at least a week. Then pull it out and read aloud and see if it all makes sense, is intriguing, and as complete as you can make it.

## MORE IMPORTANT SYNOPSIS DETAILS

Once you introduce the Main Character, describe her problem and what she wants. Show conflict and briefly describe setting if it's notable to the story (it often is). Include her motivation and don't forget to reveal the resolution. You can find many examples online for your genre. Just google! Type in "novel synopsis" then the genre, such as "young adult" and you're bound to find some sites with clear examples.

The average length for a synopsis is generally between 500-1,000 words, or two to four pages. Again, this varies, so check the publisher or agent's submission guidelines. You don't want to send a five-page synopsis to an agent who only wants two. That alone is cause for dismissal because it tells them you don't follow directions, which also tells them you're not professional. No matter how good your book may be, they shy away from writers who are lazy and do not appear serious about their career.

## SENDING ELECTRONICALLY

In most cases, you'll be sending your synopsis in an attached email. There are some agents and editors who still request snail mail, but that practice is becoming obsolete. Identify that this is the synopsis in the subject head of your email submission. Few people like to see all caps in the headings (it looks like you're screaming), but you do want the agent/editor to see it among the hundreds of other emails he gets. I will usually put it like this: "SYNOPSIS/ Title. This way, it catches their eye, they see clearly that it's the synopsis, then the title, no caps, lets them know which book it is.

In the body of the email, write a nice professional cover letter stating that this is the synopsis they requested, and end by thanking them for their time and consideration.

Again, this is usually after you've sent your query and have received the go-ahead for the rest. Some agents or editors, however, request the synopsis in an attachment along with the manuscript request. Do whatever they prefer. This goes a long way in showing that you'll be easy to work with.

**Recommendation:** Have you writers' group or Beta reader read through your synopsis before sending it out. Ask them to tell you, honestly, if the synopsis truly tells the full story in a concise and compelling way. Then take them out to lunch for their time or reward them in some other away. Remember their time is valuable, too.

**Writing Workshop:**

Write out the long version of your novel synopsis. Even if you don't use it, it's a great way to start writing out the story in a concise and entertaining (hopefully) manner.

Remember, it's often easier to cut something out, rather than trying to decide what to add in.

Good luck!

*Chapter 13*

# ROLLING DOWN THE HIGHWAY: SENDING THE QUERY LETTER

*"The road to publication can be rough, take snacks and a friend."*
*Elizabeth Hein*

Now that you know how to put together a proposal and/or synopsis, you are ready to draft your professional query letter. Query submissions are high traffic area, so it's important to stand out. In a good way. After the work you've done preparing for this essential letter of introduction, you are more in touch with your book's story and better qualified to write a top-notch letter.

A query is a business letter that introduces your book idea to an agent or editor, and serves as your "selling tool." It should be professional, interesting, and reflect the tone of your book. It is also the primary reason you sell or don't sell, your book.

Yes, there's a lot riding on this thing.

The query is your first contact with an agent or publisher *before* you send out your book proposal or the synopsis. If they like it, they will ask you to send for your proposal or synopsis. You might wonder, if you send the query first, why is this chapter *after* the ones on book proposals and the synopsis?

Because you need to have that proposal or synopsis complete and as perfect as possible *first*. Doing so helps you write a better query letter because you now know your book more thoroughly. Plus, as stated earlier, if that agent or editor responds right away to your query and asks you to send your non-fiction proposal with sample chapters, or novel synopsis with your complete manuscript, you better have everything ready to go while their interest is high. If you don't have those sample chapters done, or still slaving over that novel synopsis, they don't want to hear that they have to wait for you to finish what should already be complete.

Industry assumption is that when you send out your query, you are ready for the next step, anxious to proceed forward. If yours is a novel, they may ask for a "partial" (usually the first 50 pages) or the complete manuscript, so best have it ready and in good shape. Being prepared for what's expected in the industry is how you hook the agent or editor. This is your chance to reel them in, or that almost-caught fish will swim away towards some other fisherman's rod.

Let's get started.

## STANDARD BOOK QUERY

There are four basic parts to a query.

**The Lead:** The intriguing beginning that will hook interest.

**The Body:** A brief synopsis of the story. A short paragraph detailing the story (fiction) or book information (nonfiction).

**Your Credentials:** Notice this comes towards the end. They want to know about the book before they want to know about you. For nonfiction, mention why you are the right person to write this book. For fiction, name any published short stories or fiction contests won. If you've never published any fiction, no need to say so. There are other ways you can demonstrate your qualifications (more on this later).

**The Conclusion:** Here's where you ask if they'd be interested in seeing your proposal or completed novel manuscript. Let them know your proposal and/or synopsis is ready, and conclude by thanking them for their time.

Writing a great query letter takes time, patience, and practice. And it's definitely something you'll want to have your "people"—writer's group or writing partners—go over with their bright red pens. Remember, the query letter is your pass to get in, or keep you out. It has to be as good as you can make it.

## QUERY FORMAT

A professional query letter is single-spaced and almost always one page. However, if your book is nonfiction and is going to be lengthy, with many references and information, you could run longer and that's okay. But try and keep it no more than one and a half pages. Make it as concise as possible while including all the necessary marketing details.

## WHEN'S THE BEST TIME TO HIT SEND?

There is no real "best" time to send a query because every agent, or publishing editor, works a bit differently and you never know what's going on in their office. In addition, no matter who you send it to, yours will be among hundreds in the agent's or editor's Inbox that same day. And yet, writers still want to know which is the most favorable day, time, month, moment, to send a query. And that's a tough call. You don't know if that agent is getting ready to marry, or an editor is on vacation, or his wife just had a baby . . .

First off, you shouldn't hold off sending your query just because it's a Monday (busiest day for most), or a Friday (many take off early), or it's June or July (summertime, vacations!), or August (back to school time), or December (holidays). There will always be something in the mix so don't use these as excuses, reasons to procrastinate because you're too afraid to hit that Send button. I know, it's scary.

However, there are some obvious times you will want to hold off. National holidays are out, of course, including Jewish and Christian. Thanksgiving week, too. And yes, Fridays may not be the best. I get the least amount of emails on Friday, which tells me people do things other than work, even when they are at work. But again, you *don't know*. You can't know. Just send the darn thing when you feel it's ready. But then, make sure it *IS* ready and you're not just anxious "to get it out there." No sense in sending a query that will prompt a sure-fire rejection or worse, be ignored. You'll get enough of those anyway, to tell the truth. Don't increase those chances.

You should have a list of agents or publishers at the ready, with notes on what they are looking for, starting with the names of your "dream" agent, or publisher, on down the list. *Don't forget to find them through your *Writer's Market* or other source guide, then check their websites.

Best not send to your top choices first. Why? Because sometimes as you're sending away, you will spot something that you missed in your original query, or discover a better way of describing your book, etc. So you might want to test the waters and send out five from the middle of your list first and see what happens. Those will help you see if you're on the right track, based on responses. If you're getting rejections right away, you'll want to go over your query again and see what's apparently not working. You don't want to mess up on a chance of getting that dream agent or publisher from the top of your list.

While you are patiently waiting for responses, begin your next book, or continue to tweak your manuscript. Try not to think about your submissions being looked at "right now!" That can drive you crazy. Stay busy with other work.

If you haven't heard back from an agent or publisher after six to eight weeks, go ahead and send a follow-up email, using the subject head: **Query Status: Title**. This will let them know that you are following up on a query, and you should get a response one way or another. But not always. Some agents and editors simply don't bother responding. Still, we writers want, need, an answer, don't we? Even if it's a rejection. The standard and quick, "Not for us" or "No, thanks" is better than being ignored. But the hard truth is, you will often be ignored.

So if you don't get a response after a follow-up, move on to the next names on your list. And try to stay positive. That "Yes, I'm interested" may be just another query away.

## KEEPING THE "R" WORD IN CHECK

The decision to reject your work is a business decision and isn't about you personally. Unless of course, your query is god-awful. So while it may be because of poor delivery, it's more likely a host of other reasons. You can catch an editor on a bad day, or an agent just returned from vacation and facing a mound of catch-up work, or your query is simply missed in the maze of others and ends up far down at the bottom of her Inbox.

There are, however, a few common reasons for rejections. Some can be avoided. Others are not in your control. They are:

1.  You didn't follow their submissions guidelines. Make sure you send your work to someone who is interested in the genre of your book.
2.  They've already published, or about to publish, a book too similar to yours. Yes, I know I told you your book should be similar to a few

others, but sometimes it can be too much so. This is just bad timing for that particular agent, or publishing company, and unfortunately, there is no way for you to know that.

3. Once again, timing. An agent or publisher may think your book isn't marketable at this time. That's a perfectly valid reason to decline, but it still stings. Although you want to write a book you have a passion for, it might not be something enough readers would be interested in.

4. Your book may not be the kind they are hot on the trail for. At this time.

5. You don't have the credentials to write this nonfiction book. Or you don't have any kind of platform to help launch your debut novel. Both are reasons for you to get these things started before pitching your book. (See Chapters 15 & 16.)

6. You used "fictional novel" in your book description. Duh. Of course your novel is fiction. That's what a novel is. This may seem trivial, but agents and editors hate this misuse. It tells them you don't know any better, often prompting an instant rejection.

7. The pitch is boring. Which means so is the book.

8. Your word count for your novel is too long or too short. While you should include your word count, make sure the length is right for the category of your book. It could be a bit shorter or longer, but if your book is, say, in the range of 150, 000 words, that is reason enough to get rejected.

A great online site on queries is Marla Miller's Quick Query Critiques. Miller is an editor, author, and writing workshop instructor. She reads queries on video and critiques them. You can learn much about what makes a good query letter—and what doesn't—by watching these videos on her website. Hopefully, this will still be available whenever you are reading this book. See www.marlamiller.com, or google her name.

**FAQ - Frequently Asked Questions:**

*Q*: This book is the first of a series, should I mention that in the query letter?

*A:* Probably not. While many agents and editors do like series, they want to first see if you can write one book well enough before worrying about subsequent ones. However, if you've already written book two in the series, it doesn't hurt to mention it. But concentrate most on selling the *first.*

*Q:* Should you mention a self-published book?

*A:* Most professionals aren't interested in previously self-published books, unless they have sold very, very well. Even then, if it has nothing to do with your current book, no need to mention it.

*Q:* Can I query more than one agent in the same agency?

*A:* Not usually. If one agent rejects your work, the others probably will too (for whatever reason). However, if an agent thinks your book might interest another agent in the company, she will pass it on herself.

* A little secret: Go ahead and include the first page (only) of your book, below the query. If the query is of any interest to the agent or editor, he won't be able to resist reading further and it just might be the enticement needed to get a positive response.

* **It's** a good idea to let them know why you are contacting them. Mention any referrals, or books, or clients they represent or publish. You might want to mention this in the lead of the query to get their attention right away. If you don't have a name to drop, but have another reason to let them know why you want them, you can mention that at the bottom.

Here is one of my queries I sent an editor for *Confessions of a Not-So-Good Catholic Girl*:

April, 2008
Editor Name
Publication Address
Dear [Editor Name]:

"Life experiences with a twist of faith." This is the theme of my book, *Confessions of a Not-So-Good Catholic Girl*, a collection of stories from a baby boomer land-scape in the Midwest. It's about family. Faith. Love (lost *and* found). Parenthood.

And aging. While I weave historic events and pop culture trends throughout the book, my focus is on the relationships and human experiences that ultimately influence who we become. In my case, the trials and ultimate salvation of a rebellious Catholic girl who turns out better than most predicted. Ironically, I've been nominated for my high school's Prestigious Alumna Award—something I'm sure even God himself didn't see coming.

Some of these essays were gleaned from previously published pieces. My work has appeared in *Ohio Magazine, Sesame Street Parents, The Plain Dealer Sunday Magazine, Writer's Digest,* and others. My first book, *Rock 'n' Roll and the Cleveland Connection* (Kent State University Press, 2002), was a finalist for the 2003 Ohioana Book Award for nonfiction, and finalist for the ARSC Award (Association of Recorded Sound Collections) for excellence in research.

Because most of the stories are based in Ohio, I feel strongly about obtaining an Ohio press. I am impressed with the diversity of your titles and topics, and feel confident that your company would be a good fit for this book. This is why I am submitting my proposal to you exclusively.

I thank you for your time and consideration, and look forward to hearing from you.

Sincerely,

Deanna R. Adams

Notice three things about this query: I had a good lead tagline, "Life experiences with a twist of faith." And I used a bit of humor, "Ironically, I've recently been nominated for my high school's Prestigious Alumna Award—something I'm sure even God himself didn't see coming." If you can use humor, especially if it reflects the tone of the book, by all means use it in your query. And use the same voice in your query as you use in your book (in my case, conversational). Also, I mentioned some accolades from my previous book. I ended by telling the editor exactly why I'm submitting to their company. This shows that I did my homework and am familiar with the books they publish.

Because this book was a memoir, thus, nonfiction, I included my book proposal, which mentioned who my target audience is—baby boomers—how I would market it, and all those sections we discussed in Chapter 11.

Did it work? No.

I'm being honest here because this is not a how-to book where I claim "if you do everything I say you are guaranteed to be published." No book should ever boast that because there are no guarantees in this business. As I've said before, the book industry is subjective and the bottom line is money. *It's a business.*

I did not sell this book to a traditional publisher. But because I had a well drafted, professional query/proposal, I received many "good" rejections (yes, there is such a thing). Some agents and editors actually take the time to write you a personal note, or email, and when that happens it means you're on the right track. But it doesn't always mean you'll sell it.

This particular editor I pitched to, wrote me back saying he loved the chapters I included in my proposal, but that his company was pulling back on publishing memoir because the market was over flooded. (Ah, timing.) He then suggested a few other publishers he thought might be interested. Now that's a great rejection! All too often, however, you will receive no reason on why they passed on your book. And that will drive you crazy, but it's the nature of the beast.

It does help when you get good rejections. This tells you did your job right, your book just wasn't right for them. Consider this: Agents and editors receive some 50+ query submissions *a day*. If they like your query enough and see the potential, some will take the time out of their busy day to let you know that. They reassure you that it's strictly a business decision, it's not personal, and not a reflection of your writing. That takes the sting out and gives you encourage to keep submitting!

Now I'll share a fiction query that received favorable responses, such as several requests for the full manuscript, and ultimately helped sell my first novel.

Dear [Editor]:

What if Buddy Holly's first love really was a girl named Peggy Sue? What if she got pregnant and her parents sent her away, as often happened to unwed girls in 1957? What if that baby grew up to be a rock star in her own right, not knowing who her real father is until someone threatens to expose the truth?

*Peggy Sue Got Pregnant* tells the story of Peggy Sue Lawrence who, after a cherished love affair with Buddy Holly, realizes she's pregnant. The timing couldn't be worse. Buddy's musical career is taking off, and Peggy Sue has another full year of high school. Her horrified parents put her on a Greyhound to Cleveland to stay with her mother's sister and her husband. Peggy Sue never gets the chance to tell Buddy.

Her uncle and aunt agree to adopt her baby girl, Charlee (after Buddy's real name, Charles), only if Peggy Sue promises never to divulge this family secret to anyone—not even her future husband. Through the next few years, Peggy Sue endures her child calling another woman, "Mama," finds out about Buddy's marriage through the radio, then learns of his devastating plane crash. Meanwhile, Peggy Sue begins receiving packages by someone claiming to know her secret. She willfully ignores them as she concentrates on starting a new life. In 1963, she gets a job at WHK, Cleveland's top radio station, where she falls in love with handsome deejay Billy Mercury. Life becomes fun again with the emergence of The Beatles, exciting musical concerts, and a subsequent marriage proposal.

But everything changes when her tormentor reveals himself (and his romantic intentions) and blackmails Peggy Sue into breaking off her engagement. Soon after, her aunt and uncle are killed in a car crash, leaving Peggy Sue with a broken heart and a teenaged Charlee to raise.

When Charlee forms a band, Echo & The MissFits—the first all-female rock group of the '70s— Peggy Sue fears the publicity that's sure to come. The conflict escalates when the antagonist threatens Charlee at a gig, and Peggy Sue realizes she must tell her daughter the truth. But will this revelation shatter the good name of a rock 'n' roll icon? Will it destroy their daughter's promising career? Will Charlee forgive Peggy Sue for keeping her heritage a secret?

*Peggy Sue Got Pregnant* merges fiction with pop culture history, taking readers through the events and music that defined the baby boomer years. I'm an award-winning writer with three published books, all of which feature pop culture events. Memberships include the Authors Guild, and International Women's Writing Guild. My 115,000-word manuscript is available for your consideration.

I look forward to your response, and thank you for your time.

Sincerely,
Deanna R. Adams

This query is a bit longer than the norm because the book is a bit longer than the average 90-100,000-word novel, spanning three decades. Also note (in case you read the book) that in my final draft, I changed the real Buddy Holly character to a fictionalized version. I decided to give his character an edgier look, and also didn't want to worry about lawsuits since his widow is still alive and from what I've read, a bit litigious over his name. You do need to be mindful of such things, even when writing fiction.

Whether your query is for fiction, nonfiction, or memoir, the quality of writing is as important as the story you want to tell. It takes weeks to draft a great query and you should always, *always*, have someone knowledgeable read it over before sending it off. Better to have someone else catch a blunder before an agent or editor does. Plus, refining even a business letter helps you become a better, more concise writer.

Good luck!

**Writing Workshop:**

No one said it will be easy. Really. No one.

Before you start writing your query letter, read and study others. You can find a ton of examples online, including the highly recommended Marla Miller query critique website.

While your queries are out, start writing up your short blurb (description) about your book. Study the inside flaps of books in your genre to guide you. Read those (good) descriptions on the Amazon site. Begin thinking of the people you want to consider to write a review for the book's back cover. You want to have all these things in place for when you get your "Yes" from an agent or editor.

Now, go write a rockin' query!

*Chapter 14*

# STREET CALLED HOPE: AGENT AVENUE

*"As a writer, you can't allow yourself the luxury of being discouraged and giving up when you are rejected, either by agents or publishers. You absolutely must plow forward."*

– Augusten Burroughs

**H**OPE. It's a wonderful, exciting, cross-your-fingers kind of feeling. It pumps you up, gives you ambition, and helps you dream bigger dreams.

It can also be a big, bad tease. It opens you up to letdowns and disappointments that trigger doubts about your dreams, in this case, your book, and can be hard to take. And yet, hope is what keeps you submitting and that's a good thing. Even if you never acquire an agent, it causes you to look hard at your manuscript or synopsis or book proposal and try and see what the agents see.

## REJECTION ROW

We might as well touch on this before going any further about literary agents because it's a part of the process. The cold, hard truth is that you *will* get rejected because books are subjective, and agents are human. The only way you won't experience rejection is to never send out a submission. Or to self-publish. But *please*, DO NOT do the latter simply because you're afraid to send out your work. That's really cutting yourself, and your book, short.

Unless you've already decided to go the DIY route, you owe it to yourself to try and get your book published by a reputable, traditional publisher. Especially if this is your first, as mentioned in Chapter 10. As you begin to submit and acquire those rejections, here's another opportunity to peruse your proposal or manuscript with new eyes—an agent's eyes—and try and see what might have caused them to turn your book down. There are as many reasons as to why a manuscript gets rejected as there are books. Knowing, and accepting, that is half the battle.

## WHAT DO AGENTS DO?

Understanding the job of an agent and the world in which they live, is the first thing you need to know. Literary agents are the gatekeepers to the big and best book publishers, formerly known as the Big Six, but now is The Big Five with the merger of Penguin and Random House a few years ago. These are: Hachette, HarperCollins, Macmillan, Penguin Random House, and Simon & Schuster. However, each of these publishing companies have several imprints, and a few of those don't require an agent.

Many of these larger publishers do not accept "unsolicited material" (submissions they didn't ask for), which of course narrows your possibilities in publishing. An agent can get you, and your work, through those closed doors. It's their job to convince a submissions editor that they should buy your book. In addition, an agent can marry your book with the right publisher.

They also do more than that.

When it comes to contracts, literary agents know what publishers want and which ones are the best fit for your book. Many know the editors personally, thus, know their interests, personalities and preferences. Agents can negotiate on your behalf.

Did you know that many publishers have different contracts for writers, one for non-agented authors and a "better" one for agented authors? This can mean a higher percentage of royalties, and other important factors. However, in order for the agent to sell the book, your work must be stellar. Having a professional agent to help you enhance the quality of your nonfiction book proposal or novel synopsis can help you get it sold. They work with you so they can sell it to one of the top publishers, or a publisher that's best for your book, which can be anywhere from a small press to a university press. Keep in mind that sometimes they end up selling to a publisher that doesn't require an agent. You are still better off because they can negotiate a better contract for you since they know the business better, and can act as your liaison in all industry matters, including foreign rights.

Lastly, having a reputable agent will give you instant credibility, which is important when it comes to media attention and booksellers having your book available in their stores.

## DO YOU REALLY NEED AN AGENT?

This is a question most writers ponder some time in their writing career. With all matters pertaining to books, it's about personal objectives. The first thing you need to ask yourself is, what do I envision for this book? Do I want all of the control, make all creative decisions, including art work and book cover, and willing to put up the money it'll cost for editing, printing, design, and publishing? If that's the case, you'll want to consider self-publishing and won't need an agent. Or, if you like the idea of a small press rather than a big conglomerate, then an agent is not absolute.

Now ask yourself *why* you want an agent. Do you long for the status that goes with having an agent? Or do you most want someone to be your companion, your personal guide, on this lonely road? Do you feel you need someone to help you make your manuscript better, be your cheerleader and give you confidence in your work? (Though keep in mind, your writers' group can do that for you.) Do you want to sell more copies, get a better contract for your book? You will then want to seek an agent.

If the topic of your book is strictly a local topic, you might consider seeking a local or regional publisher, and again, won't necessarily need an agent. If you plan on publishing only one book in your lifetime (and do you really know that for sure?), then you won't need an agent.

On the other hand, if you are writing a book that has the potential for national or international appeal and want professional credibility as a writer and get paid accordingly, you should consider obtaining an agent.

A literary agent can, and should, do all the above for you.

## WHAT DO AGENTS LOOK FOR?

Professional agents are actively seeking "career writers." They want to work with authors who have more than one book in them, and already planning his or her next book, or a series of books. They want to be involved in that writer's career, and hopefully be working with the author for years, and books, to come. They look for someone who understands the business and is easy to work with. You want to be that person.

Like a marriage, or any relationship, there needs to be mutual understanding and good communication. But sometimes certain personalities just don't mesh. Both author and agent want to build a good relationship so it's best to start off by being honest with one another in terms of wants and expectations to avoid "creative or irreconcilable differences" later on. Though one can never predict the future, communication and a general respect for each other is key to a successful working relationship.

## HOW TO IMPROVE YOUR CHANCES OF GETTING AN AGENT

We've already addressed the importance of making your proposal/synopsis/ manuscript/query the best you can before submitting. That is always your best bet in acquiring an agent.

You should also become familiar with the business. If you haven't already done so, get acquainted with the book world. Join online industry newsletters and sign up on blog sites that talk about everything agents. Peruse *Publisher's Weekly,* either online or in print. "Publisher's Lunch" is an online newsletter you can get right in your inbox and will keep you up-to-date on what's going on—who's publishing what, who's changing agencies, who's buying what, etc. You'll find out the latest about agents and publishers and will often discover literary agents and publishing companies you didn't find through your other research.

Ideally, you should have some kind of "platform" before approaching an agent. This means, other published works, an active Website, speaking experience, and memberships with writers' organizations. Whether you end up seeking an agent or not, these are great advantages for when it comes to marketing your book. Being active in your local writing community is always beneficial. So get out there and attend writers' events and make some writer friends. Not only will those friendships likely be long-lasting, you are bound to find out all kinds of information through them that you might otherwise never know about.

As you research agents, you will come across the term, "simultaneous submissions." This means sending out to a number of agents (or publishers) at the same time. While some agents state that they do not "accept simultaneous submissions," it's understood that most writers will do just that. And they should. Here's why: Most agents take weeks, months, to respond (and some not at all) and if you send your query, book proposal, synopsis, manuscript to one agent at a time you'll be old and gray before you ever get the book sold. It's unfair for any agent to request that *unless* they specifically ask for an exclusive. An exclusive is a professional understanding between you and the agent, that he will be the first to read and consider the book before anyone else. This is always good news because it shows that the interest in your book is high. Be sure, however, that there is a time limit agreement, usually four to six weeks. During that period, do your part and hold back from sending it out elsewhere. If the agent hasn't responded after the agreed upon time, wait a week, then send a follow-up email asking if he is still interested. If you still don't hear anything in another week, feel free to resume your search.

I repeat: Be sure your book proposal and/or manuscript is ready before you begin querying agents so when they ask to see it, you can send it right away while they have you fresh in mind. While many don't respond quickly, some do. For example, the first agent I queried for *Peggy Sue Got Pregnant* replied within hours of my sending the query and asked for an exclusive. Had I not had my manuscript and synopsis in shape, she may have lost interest by the time it was "ready." And although that one didn't work out, it was good to know that I was in the ball park of what attracts agents and gave me confidence to move forward. Plus, because I came across as a professional, that agent is more likely to take a look my work in the future, if I decide to go that direction.

I hate to discourage you, but sometimes you never hear from an agent after sending the work *they* requested. In one case I experienced, an agent asked for a "partial" (the first 50 or 100 pages of your book), then I waited. And waited. I sent her two follow-up emails requesting some kind of response, but never heard from her again. Apparently that was her "answer." Rude? Absolutely. Frustrating? Oh yeah. But again, it's part of the biz.

## HOW TO FIND THE RIGHT AGENT FOR YOU

Once again, you need to research. Check books on agents, such as *Jeff Herman's Guide to Book Editors Publishers & Literary Agents,* and other books that list current agents. Look for those who are interested in the type of book you wrote, and their clients' titles to see if any are similar to yours. Mention those titles when you approach the agent. This shows that you have done your homework and are familiar with the kind of books they like to represent.

Also, look at the "Acknowledgments" page of the books in your category. Many times the author thanks their agent and you might find a name you didn't know about who would be perfect to pitch your book to. Query that particular agent because you already know they are interested in books similar to yours.

## WRITER'S RESOURCES

Here are some of the top current resources to use in your search for the right agent:

**Writer's Market**
**Publisher's Marketplace**
**Publisher's Lunch**
**Absolute Write Water Cooler**
**AgentQuery**
**Query Tracker**
**Preditors & Editors**
**1000 Literary Agents**

I recommend signing up for the free *Publisher's Marketplace* and *Publisher's Lunch* newsletter/daily email which keeps you updated on what's happening in the industry. Here you'll often find agents and publisher names you won't find in other sources. You can register for a paid membership of *Publisher's Marketplace* which gives more access into the world of agents, but if you don't want to spend the extra $25 a month, don't worry, you can do without it just fine.

One of my favorites in this list is *Absolute Write Water Cooler* because of the helpful forum where writers weigh in on their experiences with a certain agent or publisher. I've found the easiest way to use this site is to first google the name of the agent or publisher, along with the words, Absolute Write. Like This: "**Jane Doe Absolute Write**." When you are googling, be as specific as possible for best results.

Also, check to see if the agent is a member of the Association of Author Representatives. While some reputable ones are not, most are, so that's a consideration. If they aren't, do some more investigating to make sure they are, in fact, reputable.

## KEEP A SUBMISSIONS LOG

As you're sending off those letters, keep track of your submissions. In your log, note what you sent, who you sent it to and when you sent it. Knowing the date you sent your submission is of Major Importance. You need to know when you sent it so you know when to follow up! Make notes on all that and more, including the agent's newest clients and their books, to get a feel for what currently appeals to them.

## AVOIDING UNSCRUPULOUS AGENTS

In your excitement at the possibility of getting an agent, it's tempting to just go through the names and not dig for more information on that particular agent. This is not a time when you want to be lazy.

Once you've made your strategic agent list, check them out one by one. Rather than just go into their website, google their names and see what comes up. While many agents are on the up and up, some are not. In your great anticipation in getting an agent, don't let yourself be vulnerable. Check his or her credentials and track record. And never pay an agent to look at your work. If they ask for a "Readers fee," run for the hills. Agents must earn their pay by helping you acquire a good reputable publisher, and so, will get their standard 15% *after* the book is sold.

Also, don't pay an agent for a "quick response." There is a trend nowadays with some agents requesting money for a "rush" on their response to your submission. Some note in their websites that they "receive hundreds of queries and manuscripts weekly" (which is normal) and that it can take "several months" to respond. They then suggest that if you want your submission moved to the top of the heap for a more speedy reply, simply send a payment of a certain amount, usually $25.

Uh, no. Don't waste your money. I once queried an agent who offered that option. I decided to take my chances on the wait, even though it was snail mail and that often takes longer anyway. I still received the rejection in two weeks. Not bad for someone who didn't pay the fee for a quick response. Perhaps the agent had a slow week. . . .

Use common sense when it comes to agents. Don't let your strong desire to obtain one cause you to make bad choices. Having a bad agent is worse than having none at all. I know authors who have had agents suddenly "disappear," along with their royalty payments, and some whose agents were just poor business people and the author suffered because of it. Do your homework on them before signing on the dotted line and avoid extra heartache and misery.

## MORE ON DEALING WITH REJECTION

I'm sure you have read magazines, books, and online articles that boast the heading: How to Get, or Land, or Snag an Agent. What they really mean—but are using good marketing word choice—is that they can *help* you by providing information on how best to do that. Truth be told, even if you do everything they suggest, it doesn't *guarantee* that you'll Get, Land, or Snag an agent. This is a subjective business and there are just too many factors.

Even if you've sent your query/proposal to the right agent for your book, according to their website, there are a number of reasons it didn't get picked up and they're too busy to tell you. I listed several reasons for rejection in Chapter 13 on queries, but there are a few more specific ones when it comes to agents.

## HERE ARE THE TOP 5:

1. The agency already represents too many books in that genre.
2. Your target audience is too small. Agents want a book that will gain a large readership.
3. Your query or manuscript isn't well written.
4. Your word count is ridiculous. Which shows you're not familiar with your book's genre. For example, romance typically ranges from

70,000 to 100,000. Memoir 70,000 to 90,000, and YA is generally under 70,000 words. In other words, don't send a 150,000-word manuscript for a cozy mystery when the guideline for that genre is around 70,000. Nonfiction works are often longer, from 80,000 to 110,000 or more. My first rock book was well over 150,000 words because it was considered an academic history. However, that is not typical. Best to know the "rules" of your genre.

5. Your book follows a publishing trend that is already flooded in the marketplace, *or* is no longer popular. I've recently seen one agent post on her website, "We are currently not accepting any more books featuring vampires, wizards, warlocks and the like." And probably by the time this book comes out, the huge buzz over *50 Shades of Grey* would have died down, too. Then again, who knows? Don't write a book with the sole purpose that you think it'll sell because that's what's selling today. Remember, it takes at least a year to write it, possibly another year to sell it, still another year or more to have it published (in traditional publishing) and by then that trend will most likely be long over. Write the book you are most passionate about. Because that will reflect in the writing of it and allow you to write a better book. Plus it's a lot more fun to write what truly interests you!

While you can't control all the reasons your work gets rejected, you can control some of it. Learn as much as you can about the craft as well as the business, and become the best writer you can be. That right there can help limit rejection.

Through the years, I've talked to several successful writers who admit that they're glad their first works never got published. In hindsight, they can see the agent's viewpoint and now, as better writers, they realize it wasn't good enough and made the wise decision of not having it out in the world. And that's okay. You don't *have* to get it published merely because you've invested all that time into it. Chalk it up to practice, a learning experience. That is never a bad thing. By the time you write a complete book, you are already a better writer than you were when you began. With each book you write, whether it gets published or not, the mere act of writing and seeing it through is monumental training in becoming a more polished writer.

I know I've said this before, but it bears repeating: My most fervent advice to those who decide, for any reason, to self-publish is to have it edited by a professional editor, then vetted by someone who is familiar with that genre. Both will catch things you often miss.

And there is this: Many writers who've had numerous rejections, don't give up easy and they keep on that train of submitting. Oftentimes, they eventually do find that agent who loves their book and can't wait to represent them. *But* that's a result of a focused plan. They did not just send out their work willy-nilly. All submissions need to be targeted to the right agent to increase the chances of success.

## WHILE YOU'RE WAITING, WRITE!

The best way to deal with rejection, or the nerve-racking wait for a response, is to keep writing. Start a new book, or blog, or essay, and keep your mind off the fact that an agent is sitting (perhaps right now!) reading your work. Yes, I know you do. We all do. We stay awake at night wondering how the agent is feeling as he is reading our work. But you see, chances are he isn't because he's at a party or on vacation or reading another manuscript. There's no way to tell, so why think about it? Keep on with your life and simply hope for the best.

Yes, it is truly disappointing, sometimes even depressing, to get rejected. And the more you get them, the worse it feels. We have all been there. Even the "great ones" have known the heartache of rejection. But it's part of being a writer and the only way to avoid it would be to never send anything out. But then, that's an immediate rejection, isn't it?

We all agree that rejection sucks, but we can also learn from them too. Especially if you're lucky enough to receive a personal reply. When an agent takes time out to write a note to you, no matter how short, among all the thousands of submissions she gets, be assured that she takes you seriously as a writer. Which means you have become a professional and it's often a matter of time before you get the much anticipated acceptance. Agent feedback, despite rejection, can help you improve and make your book better. Best of all, it's encouraging and helps you not give up too easily.

## WHEN TO FOLLOW UP

Yes, the Waiting Game is Hell. That's the precise word. It is hell waiting for responses. It is hell getting rejected time and time again. It is hell having your hard work completely ignored.

Still, there's nothing like being a writer, and a lot of times, there is nothing better. Now's a good time to keep that in mind. The big question is, how long should you wait before sending a follow-up email on your query? The most common is six to eight weeks, but always check the agent's guidelines. Oftentimes they will state how long you can expect a reply. Wait at least a week after their designated time period before sending the follow-up. Then send a *brief* email to them, something like this:

Dear [Agent name]:

Hope this finds you well. I'm inquiring about the query (or partial or full manuscript) for my book, TITLE, which I had sent on July 15th. Have you had a chance to peruse it yet?

I thank you for your time and look forward to hearing from you.

Sincerely,
Your Name

Or something to that effect. If you've had a response from another agent, but really want an answer from this agent, tell him (or her) that another agent is interested in your manuscript but because he is one of your dream agents, you are holding off until you hear from him. It doesn't hurt to compliment the agent. Everyone likes to hear that they matter. Also, make sure the subject heading reads: Query Status or Manuscript Status, whichever is the case, so they know right off that you are following up on a submission. If you still don't hear from the agent in a week or so, move on, they aren't interested.

Finally, if, after many submissions (the final number is up to you), you haven't received an agent's interest, it's not the end of the world. At this point, there are still ways to get it published as described in Chapter 10. Now's the time to utilize that information.

There is also this truth: Your book may not be something that would sell a million copies. In today's tough industry, that's a real consideration. Not having a large market for that topic is one of the biggest reasons for rejections. Remember, agents main job is to represent authors and books that will attract a wide audience so that their 15% will give them a decent living.

Now cross your fingers and keep submitting!

**Writer's Workshop:**

Get started researching agents. This will take some time, so do a little each day perusing the *Writer's Market* and the online sources mentioned in this chapter. Write down your list from your number one choice "Dream Agent" to other possibilities that sound like a good match.

Then send out five from the middle or bottom of your list. Remember, you're still in the learning process of submissions and you want to see how well, or not, your query is being received. If you get a request for a submission, great! And now that you know your query must be good, send it out to your favorite candidates. If you get rejections, or no response at all, from that first batch, you should probably take a deeper look at your letter and see how you can revise and make it better.

# Part Four – Market It

*"Marketing is first and foremost about connecting."*
*– Wendy Paine Miller*

*Chapter 15*

# TAKIN' IT TO THE STREETS: PROMOTING YOUR BOOK

*"We are stuck with technology when what we really want is just stuff that works."*
*- Douglas Adams*

Ever since you thought about writing a book, you've probably heard and read a lot about the importance of Marketing. And Platform. And Branding. Now that you've completed your book and getting it ready to be published, you're probably wondering what, exactly, you have to do and how much you have to do about it all.

Throughout this time, you've been working on the craft of your book, and making decisions about publishing it. Now you need some "street cred." You need people to recognize you a writer, author, and someone knowledgeable about the book business. But first, how do you get the word out about your book and amass a readership?

## A TARGETED BUSINESS PLAN IS YOUR ROADMAP TO SUCCESS

There is a lot to know when it comes to marketing, but it'll be easier if you take it step by step. After reading these next two chapters, put together a concise plan, a strategic guide that you can follow as you prepare for your book's release.

In this chapter, we'll discuss these marketing topics:

**Platform/Brand**
**Your Website**
**Book Blurbs/Taglines**
**Book Covers**
**Book Reviews**
**Media Kit/Press Releases**

Use those time management skills you learned in Chapter 2 and make a list of things you need to do each week, each month, to get yourself noticed as a published author.

## YOUR PLATFORM

Hopefully, you've been working on your platform as you've been writing the book and have established yourself as a writer by means of a blog, website, speaking engagements, memberships with writers' organizations (particularly in your genre or field), and of course your presence on social media. Having a platform is having a ready-made audience that is aware of you, what you write, and have seen you out somewhere in the world speaking on your topic. Yes, easier said than done.

If you haven't already started increasing your visibility, you need to make it a priority before your book comes out. No matter what road you're taking to publication, it takes a while to get your book edited and ready to publish, so now's the time to get people excited about it.

That's precisely what you want. Excitement! People want to know *why* you decided to write this book, what it's about, and how the journey, so far, has been for you. Everyone loves a good story, so tell yours—as a writer. Many people dream of being a writer but don't pursue it, so they admire writers for what they do and anxious to hear how you became one. Be sure that personal story (though keep it short) is in your press kit, and in the "About Me" section of your website. You want people interested in you first, then your book. Drum up excitement *before,* as well as after, it comes out.

If your book is nonfiction, you definitely want people to see you as an expert in your subject—which indeed you should be after all the research you've done and the sources you've interviewed during the course of writing your book.

If fiction, you want them to see you as this creative person who can tell them a story that will keep them up at night.

This is all part of building your platform and having people connect you with that topic or genre. "Brand" is certainly a part of it.

## YOUR BRAND RECOGNITION

It's author association. As an author, what do you want to be known for? If you're a romance writer, what kind? Erotic or historical? If mystery writer, thriller or cozy? Demonstrate a clear and consistent image. My friend, Claudia Taller, is a writer who, as author of two books on the topic, is considered an expert on Northeast Ohio wineries. Another writer friend, Trudy

Brandenburg, is an avid kayaker and writes a series of mystery novels with that theme.

Your brand should be showcased in all the marketing you do in keeping with this identity. For example, I'm known as a pop culture/rock 'n' roll writer. This sets me apart from other writers and lets people know what I am best known for and what to expect from my books.

My business card here reflects that:

What do you notice first on this card? Probably the jukebox, which shouts rock 'n' roll. Next, there's my face and name right up top. Readers always want to know what the author looks like. Then the three words, "Books That Rock" tells you what kind of books I write, and finally, there are the book covers and titles inside the jukebox.

That's Platform. That's Brand. That's Marketing.

## YOUR WEBSITE: YOUR BULLETIN BOARD

Now that I have your mind working on how to go about becoming known as the author with a brand, let's get you a good website. Having a website isn't going to sell books, necessarily, but it will be the go-to place for people to find you, your books and where and when you'll be doing a talk or presentation.

A good website is your bulletin board. It defines who you are as a professional writer and acts as a showcase about you and your work. Your book should be featured on the "Home" page, along with your photo, a short bio (though this can be on a different page link), and info on upcoming events. You can have links to more, such as a blog, future events, and other writings, like essays and such. Since I coordinate several writers' conferences and retreats each year, I have links for those as well. Be sure to add your own social media links, and your email address so people can contact you. To see my website, go to: www.deannaadams.com.

The sooner you get your website up, the better. In anticipation of the release of my first book, I went ahead and acquired a domain name a full year before it came out, which was in 2001. I was lucky because *Deannaadams.com* was available. That's not always the case. Especially nowadays when practically everyone has a website, it's much harder to get the one of your choice. Unfortunately, there are people who acquire a group of domain names so that they can sell it to whoever wants or needs it. Take this example: Before this book came out, I thought about starting a new website, aside from my main one. A site that not only would feature this book and its contents, but also buyer information, and serve as a go-to site for aspiring authors who need to hone their craft or are looking for information on various writing topics. The obvious domain name for this would be *Writeabook.com*. But guess what? Someone owns that, doesn't use it, and is offering to sell it for a mere $49,000. You read that right. Forty-nine grand. Ultimately I decided to simply include info about this book in my *Deannaadams.com* website, and keep my "Writers on the North Coast" Facebook page for any info I want to give writers.

If possible, your best bet is to get your domain in your name (or pen name) so that it shows up on google search when someone types in your name. If that's taken, try to find one as close as you can. The domain sites will give you alternatives, too, besides .com, such as .net, .org, .us, among others. Be sure, however, that it's not something so obscure no one will find it—or remember it.

You also have to decide what hosting company you want and there are tons of those. Some well-known ones in 2015 are Arvixe, iPage, Blue Host, InMotion, GreenGreeks, and GoDaddy. Do some online research, ask other writers what they use, then determine what would be best for you. Remember, your website should represent who you are, *and* look professional and interesting.

Which brings us to Graphic Design 101. Your website needs to be aesthetically attractive and easy to navigate. If you have no idea how to design a website, by all means, invest in someone who does. You don't need to hire a big expensive company, just someone who is skilled at creating a site that's appealing. There are people who do this on the side who are quite good, so ask around. Study other author sites to see how theirs look, and the information they include. Then see if maybe you can get that same person to do yours.

Be sure that your website stays current. Update all information as it happens, such as your appearances or any book signings, or events you are doing. Keep it looking fresh and appealing.

Keeping your brand in mind, think about these questions as your website is being created:

* Upon first glance, does the website look credible, professional?
* Will people know I'm a writer the minute they go into the site?
* Does the site reflect the right tone, mood, I want to deliver? (Consider larger font and soft appealing colors).
* Will people see right way where the links are to find the information they seek? (Such as events, author bio, book information, etc..)

Another intriguing addition to your site would be linking a recorded interview or podcast. People love to see the author in action, and this can boost presentation opportunities. Consider doing a video interview with a friend, recording it and posting it up. Or videotape your book launching to add to your website. Also, post these on You Tube—another great way for people to find you.

## BOOK BLURBS AND TAGLINES

A blurb is a short paragraph or two that serves as a sales pitch. It describes what the book is about and is used as promotional materials in your press release, website, and on the back cover. These are generally written by the author or publisher. A blurb can also be an endorsement, a quote by another author or credible person praising the book. Those endorsements can also be used for all the above.

A tagline is a brief statement, description, about your book. It should be catchy, with short crisp sentences, and fit well on the front or back cover. The aforementioned "rule of three" works wonders here. Two examples:

From Joan Didion's memoir, *The Year of Magical Thinking*: "Life changes fast. Life changes in the instant. You sit down to dinner and life as you know it ends."

From Shelley Costa's mystery novel, *You Cannoli Die Once*: "Four generations of fine Italian cooking. One colorful family. And a killer with a taste for revenge."

It can also be short and punchy. As you see on the back cover of this book, my tagline is: "Your Navigation to Publication."

If you have secured an agent or publisher, you will probably get help with these, and will have your taglines and book blurbs ready to go early on. For those who are self-publishing, the time to do this is now. As you are editing/revising your book, begin drafting your description blurb and dynamite tagline so that you have everything in place when it's time to publish. Also, consider who would be the perfect person, or persons, to endorse your book, then ask if they are willing. If they are on board, make sure you establish a deadline so you're not waiting months to get these in.

A basic book description blurb should:

1. Introduce book's main character or theme
2. Create intrigue
3. Not give away too much of the story
4. Be short. Preferably no longer than 200 words

In other words, the description should include the essential information about the book in a fascinating paragraph or two. If the blurb is too long, it'll take up too much space on the back cover and will have to be shortened anyway. Also, many Internet book buyers are "glancers" and want to learn quickly if a book would interest them. They often won't take the time to read a long passage. So you might want to check out the book descriptions on Amazon to see how most are done.

**FOR FICTION:** The summary of your novel should include only the story's main plot, the hook. Sometimes you'll see a blurb end with a question (*"Will Sarah finally find happiness?"*), which can be effective in drawing readers in because hopeless romantics want the answer to that question. That's one method. The secret is to grab reader interest by enticing them through emotion.

Here is my blurb for *Scoundrels & Dreamers:*

> Rock singer, Charlee Campbell, aka Echo, cannot wait to start her new life—as Dusty's wife and mother to their newborn son. Then the unthinkable happens. Baby Dylan is taken from the hospital in the middle of the night by a woman posing as a nurse. The kidnapping soon threatens the couple's once-solid marriage, as well as Charlee's musical career. As the years pass, Charlee begins to doubt that she will ever see her child again. Little does she know, her son, now named Ben, is as close, and elusive, as her next hit record.

In just ninety-five words, the reader knows who the main character is, the central plot, then is lured in by two key sentences that build tension and create emotion: "Then the unthinkable happens," and "Ben, is as close, and elusive, as her next hit record."

That short blurb causes the reader to wonder, and look forward to, reading the book to find out what's going to happen, and how it's going to happen.

**FOR NONFICTION:** With this type of book, it's a good idea to use bullet points, as you see on the back cover of this book. (I practice what I preach.)

This should include some main features of the book. You don't want to over-crowd your back cover, so limit those bullet points to no more than four or five. At the top of the bulleted list, include a sentence on why "this book is for you!" An endorsement by another expert along with those bullets is great, too.

For nonfiction, especially, it's important to have your bio/credentials on the back cover so readers know that you are an expert in your field. A photo is nice, too, but if it takes up too much room, put the photo inside, on the last page. Better to have your all-important blurb, bio, and endorsements on the back.

## YOUR BOOK COVER

There are three important things about your book that can help or hurt sales. They are:

**Title** – Reflects the theme of your book and should be memorable.
**Front Cover** – Should be eye catching and fit the contents.
**Back Cover** – Should tell readers what to expect inside, through the blurbs and endorsements.

Go to any book store and watch people as they scan books. If the books are on display, it's the cover they see first. Of course, cover appeal is as subjective as books themselves, but it should still capture attention.

If you have a traditional publisher, the art department will create your cover. Some art directors will ask authors how they envision the cover, others will not. If you're self-publishing, you need a good book designer. It's yet another expense, but knowing how important a cover is, you need to make that investment. And it can be less than you think. There are tons of designers online, but again, do your homework. It's risky to hire someone you don't know on the Internet, but if you know of no one personally, you may have no choice. However, if you belong to a writers' organization, you may find authors who can help you. Ask other indie authors for suggestions. Once you find someone who seems credible, google the name for any complaints. If all looks good, contact them and see how professional their response is. It's a good idea to go with someone who states that he or she will give the author several chances for tweaks (requests for changes) so that you are happy with the end result.

I was fortunate when it came to this book's cover because I already knew someone I could trust. I loved the covers of my novels and so, contacted that designer, Rae Monet. She was booked up for some time and I had a deadline, so she kindly pointed me in the direction of Karen Duvall of Duvall Design. Because of the recommendation, I felt confident that I would be pleased, and she gave me a reasonable price. Costs can range anywhere from $5 to $800 or more. I suggest considering someone in the middle price range unless you find someone you know and trust.

As you research, you will probably come across a company called, Fiverr. com. This is one of those in the $5 range and can be dicey. In my research, I have found authors who did not get what they paid for (even at that amount) and others who were satisfied. It appears to be a better site for eBooks, and the price is certainly within anyone's budget. Just remember, you have to live with that cover and you want to be happy with it.

You will also need an attractive author photo, often seen at the bottom of the back cover—if there's room. If not, add it to the last page of your book along with your bio. We all want to look good in photos, especially when it's a part of your book, so you might want to hire a professional photographer to take at least one good head shot of you. Your picture should look professional and reflect a bit of personality, or coincide with your book's theme.

## ENDORSEMENTS

Endorsements should be from someone well-known in the genre or field, or has the credentials to be seen as a good source for a recommendation. When my first publisher, Kent State University Press, asked me to obtain endorsements for my book *Rock 'n' Roll and the Cleveland Connection*, I decided to approach several. A known journalist (to endorse the writing of the book), a radio executive (to validate the radio history in the book), a rock musician (the bass player for Van Halen, whose guitar tech was a source in the book), and the president/CEO of the Rock and Roll Hall of Fame and Museum (for obvious reasons). Each one gave credence to my standing as a writer and historian. The important thing is that you look like a pro and that your work is shown to be respected by others in your field. (Note: these endorsements come after you, or the publisher, sends them a galley proof of the book, which is an advanced copy, so they can peruse it beforehand.)

## GET A BOOK REVIEW LIST IN PLACE

If you have an agent or traditional publisher, you need not worry about this section since they will do this for you. However, if you plan on self-publishing, this is yet another thing you have to do if you want your book to get noticed.

Get your book made into the PDF file as soon as it's complete (and edited), so that you can begin sending it out *now* to review sites—some of which request new books three or more months before the release date. Be sure to do your homework on these since some charge a fee to review your book. Some might be worth it, some might not.

There are numerous review sites all over the Internet, yet some do little to help get your book recognized, much less sold. You want to target your market to the sites that are best for your type of book. If you're writing romance or women's fiction, google "**women's fiction writers reviews**," or whatever category you're seeking, and see what sites come up.

The most popular review sites cover all book categories, such as *Kirkus, Library Journal, New York Times, USA Today, The Best Reviews,* and *Midwest Book Review.* While these are respected publications, know up front that if you self-publish, some won't accept your book, or that you will have to pay a substantial amount. For example, as of this printing, *Kirkus* charges $425 for a standard review, though note that it *can* be good for exposure. *Midwest Book Review,* also good for exposure, is free of charge for printed copies, but charges $50 to review eBooks. In addition, some request a copy or two (to send to their reviewers) three to four months ahead of time. Meaning that when your book is done, you'll have to hold off releasing it until the book is reviewed—a tough thing for anxious authors to do!

The best thing about reviews is that you can use them in your press kit, put on your website, and anything else you do to promote your book. However, be aware that you might not get a good review (remember books are subjective).

The best advertisement comes from a feature story on you in newspapers, magazines, and online publications, which is almost always positive. Make sure to send press releases to feature editors, and depending on your subject, columnists. You will often find the greatest press attention in your hometown. Most local publications love to feature news about area writers, especially if it's attached to an upcoming event, like a book signing.

Now's the time to make a list of where you want to submit your book. I encourage you to find more of these resources on your own, but here are a few to start with. Aside from those already mentioned above, you might want to try:

*Publisher's Weekly* (The BookLife section)
*Foreword Magazine* (Book Review section)
*Armchair Interviews* (Review section)
*Indie Reader* (Note this publication charges $225 to review your book, but could be good exposure for indie/self-pub authors)
*Coffee Time Romance* (for Romance and Women's Fiction)

Remember to go into each of these sites, as well as others you find, and follow submission guidelines. Also, as a self-published or indie author, be sure to join the **Independent Book Publishers Association**, which offers many opportunities to get your book noticed, as well as events to attend, and a good networking community with other authors.

Once the reviews come in, be sure to post them (the good ones) on your website. Pluck a couple of the best quotes from those and place them, along with your book cover, on your Home Page.

## YOUR MEDIA KIT/PRESS RELEASE
**A Media Kit should contain:**

* A Press Release (letter of introduction) with book information
* Professional author photo, book cover image
* Articles on you
* Copy of the book

The press release (also called Media Release) should include upcoming book signings. Be sure to secure several so you can include that information in the release, along with your book launch party info. Your goal is to persuade journalists to do a feature on you, and producers of radio/TV shows to have you on as a guest. Not everyone will come through, of course, but the more releases you send out, the better chances you have. Note that you'll only have about a three-month window of opportunity to do this. People in the media want what's new, not what happened six months ago. So line up your "ducks" ahead of time so when the book comes out, you have that publicity wheel already churning.

Just as you did with your review list, make a list of everyone you can send a press release to. Check the names of the producers of radio and TV shows that feature authors, and those journalists who write on books and authors, or about your subject matter. Nowadays, few news organizations are open to snail mail, preferring email. However, if you're approaching book editors, they will often want a print copy of your book. Send the kit however requested.

Also, I find it best to write these all-important queries and releases in a document first, then cut and paste it into the body of the email. This makes it look professional and neat.

The following pages include a sample of one of my press releases (minus personal info).

**For Immediate Release**

Contact: Deanna R. Adams

PHONE:
EMAIL:
WEBSITE: www.deannaadams.com

## *NEW NOVEL BY CLEVELAND ROCK 'N' ROLL AUTHOR*

### *About the Novel, Scoundrels & Dreamers*

Rock singer, Charlee Campbell, aka Echo, can't wait to start her new life—as Dusty's wife and mother to her newborn son. Then the unthinkable happens. Baby Dylan is taken from the hospital in the middle of the night by a woman posing as a nurse. The kidnapping soon threatens the couple's once-solid marriage, as well as Charlee's musical career. As the years pass, Charlee begins to doubt that she will ever see her child again. Little does she know, her son, now named Ben, is as close, and elusive, as her next hit record.

From the dawn of MTV and shoulder pads, through leg warmers and grunge, *Scoundrels & Dreamers* picks up where Deanna Adams's debut novel, *Peggy Sue Got Pregnant*, left off. Charlee's story brings back beloved characters while introducing new ones, whose affairs of the heart create the inspiration from which cherished songs are made.

### *About the Author*

Deanna R. Adams is a multi-published author of both fiction and nonfiction works. She is a speaker, instructor, and award-winning essayist. Deanna loves her hometown of Cleveland, and rock 'n' roll music, and each one of her books reflect that passion and history. Her debut novel, *Peggy Sue Got Pregnant: A Rock 'n' Roll Love Story*, and now its sequel, *Scoundrels & Dreamers*, upholds that tradition.

Her first book, *Rock 'n' Roll and the Cleveland Connection* (Kent State University Press, 2002), was named a finalist for the Ohioana Award for nonfiction, and the ARSC Award (Association for Recorded Sound Collections) for excellence in research. Other books are *Confessions of a Not-So-Good Catholic Girl* and *Cleveland's Rock and Roll Roots*. Adams also contributed an article on the Rock and Roll Hall of Fame and Museum for the *2007 Encyclopedia of the Midwest*.

## *Price and Availability*

*Scoundrels & Dreamers: Charlee's Story,* Deanna R. Adams (Soul Mate Publishing, New York). Available through Barnes & Noble, and Amazon. Price: $2.99/ebook, $13.99/paperback book.

### ADVANCED PRAISE for Scoundrels & Dreamers
*Scoundrels & Dreamers* is a trip-down memory lane for music loving children of the 1980s. But the music is just a soundtrack to a darker tale about family, children, the power of love and the power of art. Great Read." **Laura DeMarco, *Plain Dealer* Arts & Entertainment Reporter**

A rollicking ride through the early years of MTV and the struggles to balance fame, family, and friendships. Women star in this novel and give us insider views into the wear-me-down, tear-me-down stresses of the music biz and the life-altering anguish for a missing child. A great sequel to *Peggy Sue Got Pregnant* and stand-alone novel in its own right. - **Nicole Eva Fraser, novelist**

### *Book Release Launch Party*
**PLACE**
**ADDRESS**
**VENUE PHONE**
*DATE AND TIME*
*Deanna will also be at:*
**LIST OTHER PLACES**
**[ADD THIS]: More Dates Coming Soon**

Notice several important things about this release:

**Contact information is right up top.**

**Title Gives Immediate Information**

**Book Info:** Use that great book blurb you have ready. A small photo of the book cover on the right hand side adds a nice visual to your letter.

**Author Bio:** Include anything fascinating or relevant about you as a writer, such as awards or other accolades.

**Advance Praise:** Here's where those advanced endorsements and reviews come in handy.

**Book Party Information:** Where and when book launching will take place, along with other talks and/or signings. This includes your **Virtual Book Party**, which you should consider. (Tips in Chapter 16.)

And here's something fun that's gained popularity. A "Q& A" with the author. Busy journalists love this added to a news release because it makes it easy for them to use in their feature or column. Some questions can be:

**What was the inspiration for . . . [BOOK TITLE]?**

**Do you have a favorite character in this book?**

**What is your writing process?**

**What's your best advice for others wanting to publish in this genre?**

Anything that gives information about your book and shows your personality is welcomed by the media. Press releases like these have resulted in my appearing on TV and radio shows, as well as being featured in articles, both print and online. This media attention ensures a successful book launching, and subsequent signings.

Another note: ALWAYS FOLLOW UP. News people are busier than ever now keeping up on social media in addition to their main jobs. They can easily get distracted after reading your release. A follow-up email a week or two later is a friendly reminder about your book and upcoming events. It can be something as simple—and short—as:

Dear (NAME):

On DATE, I sent you information about my new book, TITLE, and my upcoming event to take place on DATE at VENUE. I hope you've had a chance to consider it and I look forward to hearing from you.

Sincerely,

YOUR NAME

**Writer's Workshop:**

Begin studying other authors' book blurbs and descriptions. You can find these located on the inside flap of hard cover books, on author's websites, Amazon, and book reviews. Also note the taglines used to promote books. Follow their lead and begin writing your own. Even if you have a publisher, most times it is up to the author to write his or her own blurbs and taglines.

Understand that you'll be tweaking it over and over before it reads the way you want. Then, share with your trusty fellow writers and let them have at it before sending it out into the world.

*Chapter 16*

# MAKING FRIENDS ALONG THE WAY: SELLING YOUR BOOK

*"My friends are my estate."*
*- Emily Dickinson*

Facebook, Twitter, LinkedIn, Pinterest, Instagram, Goodreads . . . oh my! Yes, it is a bit overwhelming.

Like anything else, you will find what best suits you and your goals. You don't have to be involved in everything, especially if you're doing it only because you feel you have to and are not that interested. Full disclosure here: I am not a Twitter fan. I find it difficult to say anything in just 140 characters. (Though it's great practice to learn how to edit since every word counts.)

As a writer, however, I realize I need to be a part of the online social networks. It's a big part of the business these days, like it or not. I try and pop into many of them, briefly, but I enjoy Facebook the most. I love the regular communication with other writers, family, friends, and being able to stay in touch with those out-of-town. I love the longer posts that often tell a story. I love finding out what's happening in the community. I even love the baby and pet photos!

And *that's* how it can become dangerous. I'm sure you've heard that social media can be addicting and I believe this is true. Plus, it's yet another excuse for procrastinating writers (I know who you are) to suck up time that is best spent writing.

Being involved in social media doesn't, or shouldn't, take long at all. In fact, it can take no longer than five minutes or so to post, share, retweet, or respond to a post. It's knowing when to get off of it and back to writing.

Here's a great idea I learned from attending a class with *New York Times* bestselling author, Jonathan Maberry: Every writing day, save the last five minutes of the hour to jump into your social networks. You can spread it out during the course of the day. Maybe start with Twitter that first hour, then check into Facebook the next hour, then Instagram the next, and so on. Don't forget to **Set a Timer** or you'll get sucked in, I can almost guarantee it. Go in, post, comment, or share something. Then when that bell rings, get out and back to work. These regular virtual visits gives you a little writing break, keeps you on people's radars, and using that timer will keep you disciplined and maintain your productivity.

That one tip from Maberry helped my writing life greatly, and is yet another reason to attend writers' conferences—you'll always glean some new knowledge to take home, as well as meet successful authors and get great marketing tips.

Connecting on social media is imperative in the time frame before and after your book is released. Not only must you drum up excitement beforehand, you never know who might see one of your posts and share it with their friends. In fact, you can encourage friends to share your information.

One thing to know is the difference between a personal FB profile page and a business, or Fan page. Facebook profiles are personal, meant for people you know and socialize with. Facebook Pages are for business, in this case, your book business. You need to keep these separate, although you can post the same thing in both when it comes to book launchings or important events. Just don't mix the two too often.

You can consider using the big social media tool, Hootsuite, where, with one click, you can attach your posts to all your networks at once, even schedule when they will post. I don't use it because I like to change up my post for each individual network. Again, personal choice.

## WHAT'S THE BUZZ?

Begin the BUZZ about your book early on by letting people know you are writing a book! Start talking about it on your social media sites, and if you have a blog, write about the process, your progress, and any intriguing tale about your experience on this journey. Facebook, especially, is a great tool for promotion. Here's where you'll utilize your Fan Page that is strictly for your book platform, or for writers who want to be encouraged by your progress, or learn something from your writing life. You can then measure the responses, or lack of, based on likes and comments. Then tweak accordingly.

Even if your book is old, find a way to keep it alive in readers' minds. For example, you can post on an anniversary of a book's release, or when the book becomes available in a second edition, or another format, such as an audio book. Create opportunities to make potential readers know about your book without looking like you're simply "selling" it. This takes a bit of creativity, but it also gets the promotion wheels turning.

For instance, I have discovered there are many people who cannot get enough of cute animals and babies on Facebook. If you can find a way to work one of those pics into your post, by all means, do it. You'll be surprised at the amount of responses you get.

Here is an example of what I did when "Confessions" came out as an eBook, a few years after the original print book. My cat, Mojo, happened to be lying on the floor one day as I was getting my books lined up for a talk. I snuck a copy under his paw, snapped the picture and posted this on Facebook with a fun caption:

"It may be an eBook now, but hands off my print copy! I still have a couple more chapters to read, though, I wasn't crazy reading about that other cat, Tigger. I always thought Mom liked me best. But I must say the story titled, "I Was a Teenage Hitchhiker" was a hoot!"

This was an amusing way to get the word out, without my screaming "buy this book!" Notice I snuck in a little tease about a couple of stories in the book, too, for good measure.

Another fun thing authors are doing to get their book audience involved is posting different mock-up book covers on social media and asking friends to choose which one they like the best. Readers love this. If you have a publisher, they will do this for you. If you are self-publishing, you'll have to do it yourself. There are many online companies that offer a variety of mock covers to choose from, and most are inexpensive. It also helps you decide the best cover to generate reader attention.

When it comes to connecting with people on social media, please remember: Interact with other people and be involved in their posts. Comment, retweet, and "Like" their posts and comments (only if you really do, "like" of course) just as you want them to do with you.

Share fun, positive photos and show some personality. Be entertaining. Don't use Facebook strictly to pump up yourself and your book. And please, don't post when angry, vengeful or drunk. We all know those who do. Don't be that person. Always show the professional writer that you are, even on your personal page.

## TO BLOG OR NOT TO BLOG

If you already have a blog and it's been successful for you, skip what I'm about to say. Which is, blogging is not for everyone and sometimes it's just too time-consuming. That said, if you've never tried blogging, it might be a good idea to start one if your book is coming out soon. Blogging is still relevant in 2015 and I encourage you to try it.

There are thousands of blogs out there, and competition for a steady following is stiff. I recommend "guest blogging," which is posting a blog on someone else's site. This has become popular with authors as it gives you the opportunity to reach a host of new readers. There are various rules and protocol depending on the site. Research to find which ones welcome guests, or better yet, ask other writers and authors with a blog if you can participate.

This is not to say that I blog with any regularly, whatsoever. For me, it takes up too much time that I need to write for a living, as well as work on the book I'm currently producing. It's even harder to keep up when it comes time to promoting a new book. Yet, that's precisely when you need to do it. Blogs are a good way to gain readership, which will prove helpful when your book is released. I have heard rumblings lately that blog interest will eventually die down. That should not be surprising since the virtual world is constantly in flux. One thing to remember: As an author, you will be required to keep up on all the online trends and changes.

If you are new to writing a blog and want to start one, there are a few things to know:

1. Like all social media, be consistent with your postings.
2. Your blog should have a theme (something I didn't do with my first blog back in 2007). That theme should be relevant to what you write and universal enough for readers to be interested.
3. Your blog should have a place where readers can sign up so they can receive it in their inbox (This is especially important when your book is ready to come out)
4. Get your audience involved. Encourage them to comment by asking questions.
5. Be careful of what material you post online. Many publications consider blog posting "published" so if you post an essay, then send it to a magazine, they might consider that an already published work. That goes especially for writing contest entries.
6. Having said the above, it's a great idea to post excerpts from your book, before and after publication, to increase interest and get people talking.
7. Study successful blogs and see how they do it as far as theme, content, appeal and post regularity.
8. As mentioned, try some guest blogging. Ask other bloggers to feature you on their site, and you return the favor. You will gain readership from them you could never get on your own, and visa versa. A win-win for everyone.

While online connections are vital to your success as an author, there is still nothing like the personal touch. When it comes to book sales, you'll sell more when people get to know you on a personal level.

## SELL YOURSELF FIRST

My number one truth in book promotion: SELL YOURSELF FIRST. If people like you, they are more likely to buy your book. It's as simple as that. When you give a talk and people enjoy your personality, like how you present yourself, they'll stick around at the end to meet you and will most likely purchase your book. Believe me, you will sell a lot more copies this way than sitting at a table in a large book store.

You need to become visible. When you have a book coming out, this is no time to be shy. Meet and socialize with other writers by frequenting book festivals and author signings. Make friends with librarians and booksellers. These are your people. They are the ones who will be your cheerleaders, help promote you and your book, and oftentimes serve as the conduit in getting you "gigs." For instance, fellow authors can tell you who to contact or connect you with their own contacts. Managers of bookstores and librarian service coordinators, who know you, are happy to have you do a reading or book signing in their store. Before your book comes out, make some phone calls and begin to schedule author talks at book stores, libraries, organizations, book clubs, etc. Anywhere there are writers and readers, you will want to be.

Which means you will need to become a good public speaker. Ah, yes, now comes the part you probably have been dreading. But trust me, I am here to guide you by the hand and lead you through that scary world, and soon you'll be having the time of your life. That's right. Public speaking is fun! Once you get the hang of it.

## PUBLIC SPEAKING

No doubt you've heard that old adage: "The Number One Fear among people is Public Speaking." That may be true for some, but not all, and belief in that saying only makes it scarier. You really have nothing to fear but fear itself. How's that for another worn cliché?

It comes down to confidence and experience. They go hand in hand—the more experience you gain, the greater confidence you'll acquire.

If you are truly scared out of your wits about speaking in front of a crowd, I suggest you join a Toastmasters International near you. This organization was formed for those like yourself, and has a terrific track record of success. Not only will you learn to be a good public speaker, but those friends you meet in the organization will be that many more friends who may buy your book!

Besides personal appearances, you'll want to give good interviews on radio and TV, so having some speaking experience beforehand will make a big difference. Start small. Practice reading your work in front of the mirror first. Get a feel for how you look and sound. Don't be rigid. Try and relax as much as possible and *smile.* Try and feel, or at least appear, confident.

Don't forget that having written a nonfiction book, you are considered an expert on that topic, or if fiction, you are a creative storyteller. You might want to begin your talk by telling the audience something they didn't know that might surprise them. Or start with a lively anecdote, witty quote, maybe even deprecating humor if your talk is to be of that nature. Include a bit about yourself and how you came to write the book. Bottom line: Get their interest right away. Show some personality. Be yourself.

I remember the first time I spoke to a large group. I was naturally nervous, and so, with my notes—word by word—in front of me, I read from that "script." Though I did look up from time to time and smiled at the audience, I sounded all too serious and showed little personality. I knew I had to come across as an expert and professional person, which is true, but I forgot to show the audience a bit of *me.*

One thing I did learn in those early days is that people *want* you to do well. When you first reach the podium, look out at the crowd. Many will be smiling, anticipating what you have to say. Smile back at them, even if you are nervous. Smiles give good room energy. Use your nervousness and turn it into energy. When I feel anxious in front of a crowd, I draw from that nervous energy and use it to drive up momentum in the room. If you appear friendly and confident—even when you're not—the audience sees you as a high-energy, enthusiastic person, so this works in your favor. Try it, it works.

As soon as possible, take a public speaking class, read a few books on the topic, and PRACTICE speaking out loud. By the time your book comes out, you'll look like a pro.

## THE BOOK LAUNCH AND OTHER SIGNINGS

Okay, now that you have all the background information on making friends online, meeting people at various events, and speaking to a group, you should be more than ready for the big day. Your LIVE book party. Although you may have done a virtual book launching the day of release, I think a live party is a lot more fun. Of course for this, you need to have print books, and so, another reason it's to your benefit to offer your book in print as well as an eBook. As I mentioned, chances are you'll sell more books when you are out and about, talking to people about it. And this way you are satisfying both sets of readers—those who only read books on eReaders, and those who are faithful to print books.

Many new publishers are offering titles as an eBook only for the first six months or so before making it available in print. There is good logic in this since you can then expand the time frame for marketing your book. You can have a virtual launching first, be involved in many of the social media networks, then do again when it comes out in print and make personal appearances with talks and readings.

However, this might not be a good choice for you. Because I do a lot of presentations, speak at many different functions, I need to have print books at the ready. When my debut novel was sold, my publisher was one of those who always did eBooks first, then print months later. I emailed her and asked if she would please consider making the book available simultaneously in both print and electronically upon its release and explained why. She accepted my request and changed my contract. So don't be afraid to negotiate if you feel strongly about something.

Now you must decide where to hold your party. Setting is important and you want somewhere that's easy for people to find, and perhaps coordinates with your book's theme. If your book is fiction, try and book a place that is similar to the setting in your novel. If it's nonfiction, perhaps a venue that is featured in your book. For *Rock 'n' Roll and the Cleveland* Connection, I got lucky. By the time I'd completed the book, I knew a lot of people in the industry, and they were more than happy to work with me on putting together a real rockin' party. Mine was the first book on that history and included stories on deejays, musicians and clubs spanning four decades. So I, and my marketing manager, sent press releases to all the obvious people and as a result, I received great press and appeared on the major local TV networks and radio stations.

And where was the party held? At the Rock and Roll Hall of Fame and Museum. Perfect.

Other authors I know did similar things. Claudia, the woman who writes books on wineries, held hers at a popular vineyard. Trudy, the Kayak mysteries author, hosted her launch parties at stores and events for like-minded sports lovers. Another author I know wrote a book on genealogy and so, had her launching at a historical society.

The setting is just one aspect to consider. You want to appeal to your audience's emotions. Make them feel a part of it by creating an exciting atmosphere. Make this an "Event." Make it fun for everyone. For *Peggy Sue Got Pregnant*, I hired a deejay who played all the song titles from the book's chapters. The songs took people back to the '60s and '70s when the story took place and had them all reminiscing about their own lives. At the launch party for its sequel, *Scoundrels & Dreamers*, I held this at a popular restaurant/bar because that was a setting in many scenes in the book. I had the bartenders offer two specialty drinks that night: The "Peggy Sue" Martini, and the "Scoundrels" cocktail. Did I sell a lot of books at those launches? You bet I did. I also sold several copies of my other books, too, because I was wise enough to bring those as well.

Get the idea?

Your book launching party is where you'll most likely sell more books than at any other time, so I suggest you don't do giveaways at this event. Why? Because when people take the time and effort to attend your book party, they are there not only to have a good time, but also to buy your book! Don't sell yourself short. Giveaways are best left for your virtual party to help promote them online, or down the road when sales are lax and you need to pump up more interest.

Hopefully your press release will do its job and get you good notice in local media and online so people other than family and friends will attend your book launching and signings. Focus first on local, then branch out and promote your book outside your area. Anywhere there is a market for your book, you should be a part of it. Going on vacation? Google bookstores in that location or any other place you can do a talk or signing. Make a phone call, talk to the manager about having you. As soon as you book an appearance, that's the time to get that press kit out to the local radio or TV station.

As a published author, you're making friends wherever you go and online. You and your book are becoming known to those people, as well as the people *they* know. That's how it works. And there is no time-limit on that. Years after the initial release, there will still be opportunities to sell your book. For example, one of my Florida friends happened to be on a boat one day and met the program director of the local rock station. She mentioned my first book and he was intrigued. She gave me his name and number and I followed up on that connection by calling him and asking if he'd be interested in my being a guest on their afternoon show. *And* because I knew I could write off the trip as a business expense, I suggested doing this in person and he was thrilled! I then immediately made a call to their local Barnes & Noble, told the manager I was to be on the radio the weekend of . . . and got a booking. NOTE: When you tell owners or managers that you'll be on the radio, who wouldn't want you to mention their business?

In addition, I contacted the local Guitar Center (remember, think outside the box) and had a signing on the Friday night of my radio appearance. At the end of the radio interview, the deejay told the audience where I would be signing books that weekend, and *Viola*! Success.

Plus I managed a vacation out of it, too.

After you launch the book, it's generally up to the author to keep that interest going. When it comes to media and booksellers, your book has the best chance of publicity during its first three months. After that, you have to get creative. Do a promotion on an anniversary that coincides with your book or its theme, or of the release date, or anything in the news that comes up that you might connect to your book. Or you might try this: Collaborate with another author and create an exciting event. The wine author, Claudia Taller, and I put together an event called "Rock and Wine Party." It was held at one of the vineyards mentioned in her first book, with a popular local band that played for the crowd. She and I each did a talk about our books and how they came to be, and guests stayed on to enjoy the music. Between the wine, music, and friendly authors, the mood was right for engaging conversation and yes, purchase of books.

Hosting an event with another author means double the pleasure, double the fun, and often double the sales. Readers get a two-for-one opportunity to meet more than one author, purchase a couple autographed copies (we used the "makes great gifts" sales approach) and have fun in the process.

Caution: Never, ever, *expect* a big crowd. That's setting yourself up for disappointment. There are too many factors involved, so you never know. If you go with the mindset that you will get some exposure, meet a few new people, and have a nice time, you'll leave feeling less discouraged about small attendance and sales.

We all dream of major lines at bookstores and author events, but the truth is, unless you get advance press on it, you may be sitting there all alone a time or two. While the manager will book your appearance, it's mostly up to you to promote it. I learned that through experience.

For example, I had been lucky with my first few signings after my big Rock Hall book launch. The stores were enthusiastic in advertising me, helped by the fact I had just been on radio and TV. They posted signs announcing my upcoming arrival, and placed a stack of my books at the front of the store.

That can spoil an author, especially one new to the business. By the time the fourth or fifth signing came along, I had assumed (*never assume!*) that the marketing would be done for me. My first clue was that there were no signs advertising me or my book in the window as I approached the store, which was in a large mall. The second clue was when I met the manager and she guided me to the back of the store (right next to the restrooms) where I was to sit at a small table with my books. The only ones who would see me would be small children needing to go potty, and those with bladder emergencies . . .

Here is where an author needs to be a little assertive. After all, you are there for sales and don't want to waste yours, or their time. I smiled, sweetly, at this manager and gently suggested that perhaps it would be better if the table was up front at the entrance of the mall. She looked at me as if this had never occurred to her and readily agreed.

Still, there was no sign, not even on the table, so although my books were there, one customer asked me where she could find the latest Stephen King novel. Sigh.

From then on, I began doing more promoting of my signings, and always bring some kind of sign about me and my books. Yet, even with this, you shouldn't expect to sell a lot of books at a place where there are thousands of other books. Your best bet—always—is selling books at your events and targeted presentations. And no matter where you are, be sure you are friendly and appear approachable.

**Sell yourself first and the book sales will follow.**


## VIRTUAL BOOK LAUNCHING

These are practically a must nowadays in terms of promoting a new book. It can give you exposure from people all over the world, something you could never do outside the Internet.

Not only can you do this at the time of your book release, you can do it years later for an "anniversary" of the book's publication, or if your book is getting another edition.

### Party like it's 2015!

Once you get a release date, you'll need a Facebook Fan page. Set up an "Event Page" with all the virtual book launching details. Use an attractive photo of yourself, a "Cover Reveal!" and a few words about you and your book. Here you can certainly offer a free book, and maybe another prize or two. This might be a free book to the first to make a comment during your virtual book launch, or a random pick. Pump up the event on Twitter, Facebook, and other social media sites and online groups and invite everyone.

To kick off the event, begin with a good conversation starter. Or perhaps open with a video of yourself reading a *short* excerpt of the book. Choose one of the best. You want to get your fans excited!

It's a good idea to join in other author's virtual parties beforehand to see how they do it. This might give you even more ideas.

## AUDIO BOOKS

Here are yet other avenues to pursue in marketing your book. Nowadays people who love books often don't have enough time to read as often as they'd like. Yet they still want to get their book fix. In addition, there are those who don't care much for reading, but love listening to stories. Others may love books, but struggle with slow reading, dyslexia, or are blind. This drives all kinds of people to an audio book.

An audio version of a book is a whole different experience, allowing readers to listen to a book while driving, walking, cooking or working out—any way they can enjoy the book while doing something else. So naturally, it's another opportunity to get more people to buy and read your book. Try and have it available in this format at the same time as your print and eBook, so it can create additional sales across the board.

You also have to decide, if nonfiction, who will be the narrator, you or someone else who might do it best. If fiction, you need to hire people who "sound" like how you envision your characters. If you have a traditional publisher, your agent or editor will get your book into an audio version. If that option isn't mentioned in your contract, bring it up! If you are self-publishing, you'll need to do some research and figure out how best to get your book available in audio.

## MAKE A BOOK TRAILER

This is something you can do yourself however you publish your book. Book trailers are a fun way to get your book noticed because people love visuals.

You might want to take a class or workshop on putting it together. Or type in "Make Your Own Book Trailer" to find many sources to guide you through the process, including You Tube, which you can then post on when finished.

You can use your book trailer for all kinds of online promotions by having it on your website, in your newsletters, your virtual media kit, and so on. A video of your book can bring exposure to a vast audience and add interest and attention to your book through action and music—two things most everyone loves. Study other author's trailers and determine how you can make yours just as good, if not better.

## SOCIAL MEDIA IS FICKLE

As we all know, social media is bound to change through the years. What's happening online right now may be obsolete by the time your book comes out. For example, just a few years ago, My Space was *THE* space. Then came Facebook, then Twitter, then Tumblr, Instagram and so on. Who knows what will be next? Authors need to keep up with it all, but you don't have to be involved in it all, just find what works best for you.

No matter what your chosen social media avenue is, it won't necessarily generate a big increase in book sales because, as I mentioned, your best bet is still and probably will always be personal appearances. But it will get your name out there, and your book the kind of exposure you can't get elsewhere. And that's essential to any author. I have sold several books through Facebook because I have a good following there, who also have their own followers. When you build excitement about your new book and someone can't make an event or signing, oftentimes they will private message you, or email you, and ask to send them a signed book, which you should do immediately after you get their check, or once they purchase through Paypal.

Don't fret too much if someone doesn't buy your book at a signing. If you have started up a dialogue with them—personal connection—they will remember you. Let me give you just one example of how this can work.

One summer I had a book table at an outside event called "Art in the Park." I was discovering that this is not always the best place to sell books when you're competing with beautiful paintings, handmade jewelry and other fancy wares. I was beginning to get discouraged when a woman suddenly walks briskly towards me with a smile on her face. She reached my table, picked up one of my titles and said, "I want this book." I thought to myself, "*This is the quickest, easiest sale I ever made!*" I then learned that the sale had actually been made months earlier when she said that we had talked at another signing, but she didn't have the money to buy it then. When she saw me at the fair, she did have money and enthusiastically bought my book.

So just because someone doesn't buy your book at one of your events doesn't mean they never will. Some will head home and buy it online. Either way, you make the sale and oftentimes it's because they were impressed with you as well as your book.

## FINAL MARKETING TIP

When your book first comes out, you need some heralded reviews on Amazon, Barnes & Noble, and Goodreads. Just as you made a list of professional reviewers, have ready a few family members and friends who will read your manuscript or ARC in a PDF file beforehand, and will post a review before its release. Time is a factor in everyone's busy world, so make sure you give it to them in plenty of time for them to read and write up the review. Then take them to lunch or dinner in appreciation. And don't forget to gift them with a signed copy of the book.

Also, when someone contacts you to tell you how much they enjoyed your book, ask them to please post a review on those sites. If they loved the book, they'll be more than happy to do it and it will add more positive reviews.

What if someone posts a bad review? As hard as those are to read, if it's only one or two, the good ones will offset the not-so-good ones and probably won't affect sales. If you get a lot, however, and have self-published, consider pulling the book, revising it with a different cover, maybe a different title, and re-publish it. Chalk it up to a learned experience. You are now a wiser, better writer.

A stream of bad reviews is usually the cause of bad, or no, editing, and inexperience as a writer. Remember to attend those classes and conferences to become the best writer you can be, hone your writing skills, and have your work vetted by a professional.

Even if your first book doesn't sell well, your next one should sell better because more people are now aware of you as an author. The biggest thing to remember is that communication with others and personal connections will always be the most effective way to promote.

So get out there. Be visible. Attend events where you can meet other writers, such as book talks, conventions, author signings and so on. **Be a part of the writing community**. Especially in your own hometown. It's the best advice I can give.

It's about *Making Friends*.

## Writer's Workshop

Purchase a few folders you will use for your promotional ideas and contacts. Get colorful ones, or ones with your favorite animals, or scenery, etc.. Something just for fun, that makes you smile as you go through all your hard work.

Stuff one folder with all your marketing ideas—what you plan to do to kick start your book's fan base. Another can contain articles and advertisements of places and people you want to know about, to contact for future book signings, presentations, or upcoming events you want to be a part of. Another folder can include information on all the online ways that will help get your book noticed.

Keep a marketing calendar on your marketing efforts, and when you contacted people, so you know when to follow up. Always present a professional and positive attitude and people will remember you, in a good way, when it comes to future events. Keep smiling!

# AFTERWORD

*"I just knew there were stories I wanted to tell."*
**– Octavia E. Butler**

So now you know what it takes to write a book. Still want to do it? If you're a real writer, you will say yes! If not, that's okay too. At least you know now that authors are a hard working group of people who love what they do and willing to work hard to achieve their dreams—and goals.

## NOW IT'S UP TO YOU

I use the term, GPS, in this title because it serves as a map to guide you on where, and how, to begin, and will lead you to where you want to go. Your "navigation to publication" indeed. While this book covers a lot of territory, there is always more to learn. I encourage you to read additional books on the topics addressed here, and of course take those classes and workshops. The publishing world is constantly changing, and what works today might not work tomorrow. However, much of the content in this book are the basic nuts and bolts of the industry that will never change. My hope is that this will be a good resource for you to refer to for years to come.

**Remember this: Writing and Publishing is a Business.** I've bolded that sentence because it's something you need to always be aware of. You must be business-like, professional, yet show some personality in all dealings pertaining to you and your work. In everything you do, write, and say, in your communication—be it with agents, editors, publishers, and book buyers—it all comes down to you and how you present yourself.

Remember, too, that as a published author, you need to go further than your original destination. Keep your finger on the pulse of the book industry if you want to succeed now and in the future. Like any business, attend business seminars to learn what you need to know in today's current marketing trends.

Most of all, if you have passion for your book, there is no telling how far you will go!

I leave you with this classic, and absolutely true, proverb:

*"Anything worth doing is worth doing well."*

**Hope you enjoyed the trip and see you at your book signing.**

# ABOUT THE AUTHOR

**DEANNA R. ADAMS** is an award-winning writer, speaker, instructor, essay-ist, and author of both fiction and nonfiction works. She is a 2009 recipient of the Ohio Excellence in Journalism Award and her first book, *Rock 'n' Roll and the Cleveland Connection,* was named a finalist for the 2003 Ohioana Award, and the ARSC Award (Association for Recorded Sound Collections) for excellence in research.

Her novels are *Peggy Sue Got Pregnant: A Rock 'n' Roll Love Story* and *Scoundrels & Dreamers.* Other books include *Confessions of a Not-So-Good Catholic Girl* and *Cleveland's Rock and Roll Roots.*

Deanna is an instructor at Lakeland Community College, the Cuyahoga County Libraries, and on the advisory committee of *Literary Cleveland.* She is also founder and director of the Women Writer's Winter Retreat and several annual retreats and conferences, including the longstanding Western Reserve Writers Conference. She lives in Northeast Ohio with her family. **Visit Deanna's website at www.deannaadams.com for information on events and appearances.**